I0817454

What a Building Does

What a Building Does

The Hoosier Modernisms of Evans Woollen

Phillip Cox
and
Niall Cronin

Indiana
University
Press

EXECUTIVE PROFILE

Architect Sees Duty to Help Home Town

By CHARLES VAUGHAN
Business Editor

Evans Woollen III says his desire to be an architect dates back to his "sand pile days." As a child he was always building something. From his castles — in the sand and in the air — has evolved the architectural firm of Evans Woollen and Associates, 604 Ft. Wayne Ave.

His office is practically at the base of the first 30-story, twin tower apartments of Riley Center, downtown redevelopment project. Although he had no part in designing it, Woollen cheers the fact that it is developing.

"It is the greatest visual and social stride in the heart of the city since the World War Memorial plaza was laid out in the 1920s."

Woollen is a registered architect in both Indiana and Connecticut. He has two degrees from Yale—bachelor of arts and bachelor of architecture. Obviously, he could have remained in the East by joining a firm there. Why did he return in 1955 to his home town to start his own practice?

"I felt an obligation to help out," he says. "Indianapolis needs to keep a few sons at home—those with an appreciation of our historical past and an understanding of our yearnings for the future."

ARTISTS DEPENDS ON A REGION

"I also came back because Indianapolis is a good-sized city that needs help in its growth and because an architect needs a region in which to work.

The NEWS Photo, William Palmer.

Evans Woollen III, "Indianapolis needs to keep a few sons at home."

When a civic auditorium was being seriously considered some time back, he tried to encourage the city to sponsor an international competition for plans. "This way," he explains, "we would have had 500 ideas instead of five."

"A good outside firm offers stimulation to the Indianapolis architect," he says, "and some-

floor levels and there will be no aisles in the main auditorium because of the use of continental seating. This means seats are 40 inches back to back, allowing plenty of leg room and space for late arrivals to get to their seats without others having to rise for passing room.

Turkey Crop Down, Prices at Farm Rise

Indiana turkey growers took a big "slice" out of their production this year but there are plenty of birds at reasonable prices for consumers.

Output is 3,265,000 turkeys, Purdue University agricultural statisticians report, down 20% from last year.

Nationally, the output was cut 15% from the previous year with production in 1962 placed at 91.8 million birds.

Prices at farms in Indiana have gone up an average of about 4c a pound above last year but retail prices are expected to be about the same as in 1961, because of competition.

Scattered price information from around the state indicates a range of 29c to 45c a pound.

Growers in Indiana and other turkey producing states took a financial beating last year by overproducing in anticipation of government action to peg prices at a high level.

But the action fizzled following a referendum of growers who decided to fight the price problem in their own way — by cutting production in 1962.

INDIANA SECURITIES

-November 19-

Stocks and bonds quotations supplied by members of the National Association of Securities Dealers.

"Decimals" Are 8ths

STOCKS

	Bid	Asked
ALC Finance 5% pfd	91	...
Altamil Corp com	5.1	6
*Am Fletcher Nat Bank	50	53.4
American Income Life	8.2	10
Am Rubber & Plastic	21.2	23.2
Am States Ins com	27.4	29.4
Am States Ins $1.25 pfd	24.3	...
Am States Life	8.6	10
Am Sec Life	9	10.4
Associates Life	4.7	5.7
L S Ayres com	34.4	37.4
L S Ayres 4½% pfd	93	...
Ayrshire Collieries	39.4	40.4
Bankers Life Insurance	1	1.3
Bobbs-Merrill 4½% pfd	75.4	...
Buehler Corp com	7.1	8.3
Central Indiana Gas com	19	20.6
Central Soya	28.5	29.4
Chamber of Com Bldg com	7	...
Circle Theater	32.2	...
Citizens Tel Co com	12.4	...
Citizens Tel Co 5% pfd	97	...
College Life com	54	50
Commonwealth Ln 4% pfd	78.2	.
Consol Water com	15	16.4

St[...]

NEW [...] stock ma[...] ahead in [...] pushing [...] fourth st[...]

Gains [...] were fra[...] to $1 or [...] liberal sc[...]

The w[...] fairly go[...] observers[...] some kin[...] gains ma[...] rally. Th[...] ket holid[...] Thanksgi[...] expectati[...] market.

In a [...] Chrysler [...] gain, For[...] eral Mot[...] and Ame[...]

ST[...]

Dow Jon[...]
30 Industri[...]
20 Railroa[...]
15 Utilities
Standard
'500' .....

"[...]
Mid-
Morn[...]

—A—

AbbottL
Admiral
ABCVend
AirReduc
AlcoProd
AllegLud
AlliedCh
AlliedStrs
AllisChal
AlumLtd
Alcoa
AmAirlin
AmBosch
AmBdPar
AmCan
AmCBarge
AmCyan
AmElPw
AmMFdy
AmMot
AmNGas
AmStd
AmTelTel
AmTob
AmViscose
AmpexCp
Anaconda
ABCVent
ArmcoStl
Armour
AshlOil
AssdDryG
AssocInv
Atchison
AtlCstLine
AtlRefin
AvcoCorp

—B—

BaldLima
BaltG&E
Balt&Oh
B&Ostp
BellInt
Beckman
Bell&How
Bendix
Benguet
BethSteel
Boeing
BorgWarn
BriggsMf
Brunswk
BuddCo
Burlind

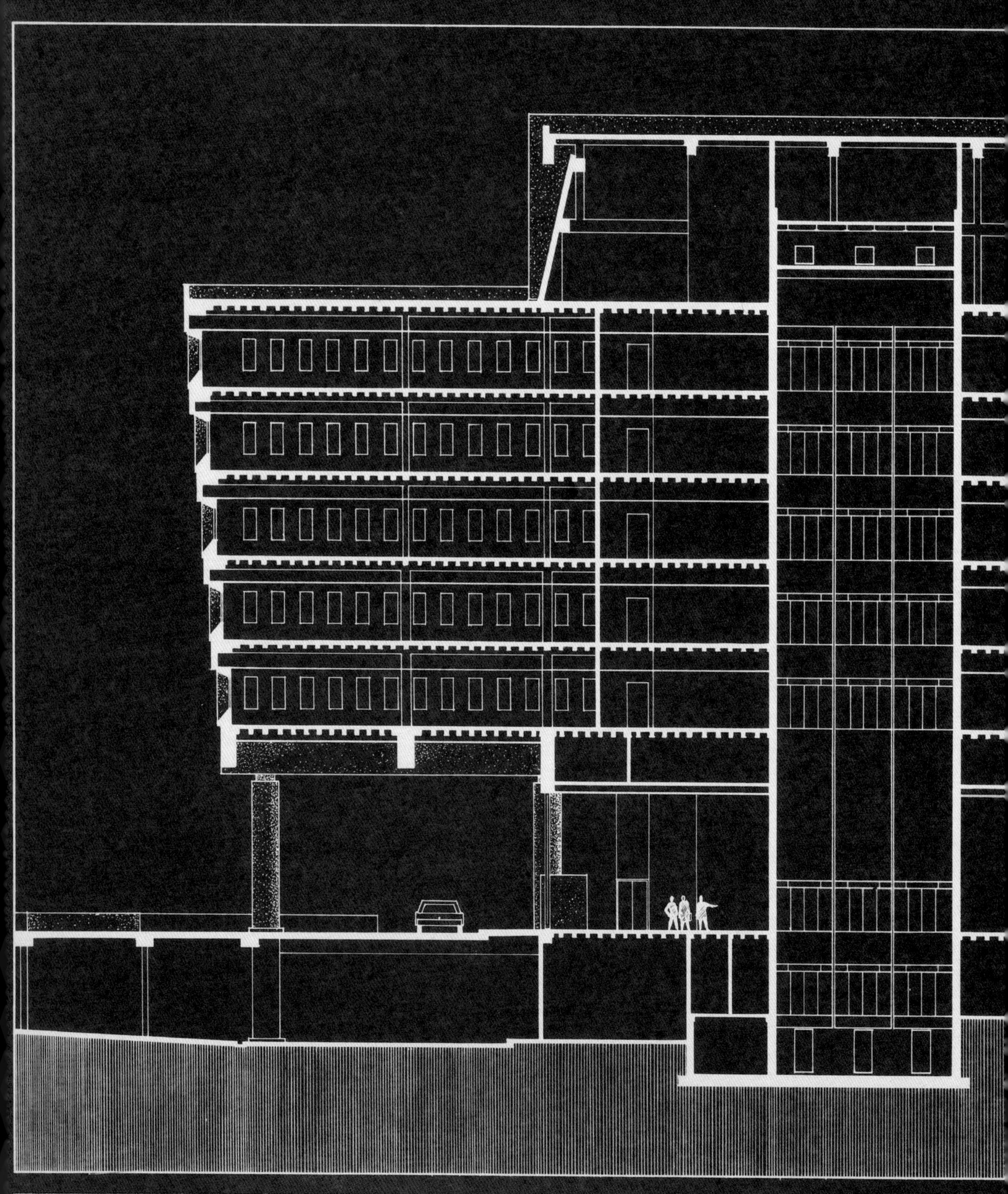

TRANSVERSE SECTION

This book is a publication of

Indiana University Press
Office of Scholarly Publishing
Herman B Wells Library 350
1320 East 10th Street
Bloomington, Indiana 47405 USA

iupress.org

Unless otherwise noted, photographs are by Niall Cronin.

First Printing 2025

Cataloging information is available from the Library of Congress.

ISBN 978-0-253-07410-2 (hdbk.)
ISBN 978-0-253-07412-6 (ebook)
ISBN 978-0-253-07411-9 (web PDF)

Pages iv–v
Indianapolis News, November 16, 1962.

Central Library.

Pages vi–vii
Minton-Capehart Federal Building section.

St. Thomas Aquinas Church.

Pages viii–ix
Woollen with Barton Tower resident, ca. 1967.

Contents

Foreword

Steven Mannheimer

I met Evans Woollen in 1982 when I began writing weekly columns on art for the Sunday edition of the *Indianapolis Star*. The managing editor, a wonderful man named Lawrence "Bo" Connor, told me to expand my "beat" to include architecture. He believed the newspaper, then the city's most public platform of information, should critique the most public form of art: architecture. Despite my trepidation, Bo assured me I could do this, that I was smart enough to read some books and interview some architects. Evans – and everyone used his first name – was my third interview, based on recommendations from the first two. ("Of course you should talk to Evans.")

Always busy, Evans was, nonetheless, generous with his time and intelligence, if occasionally impatient with my shaky grasp of his profession. Later I earned his respect for my insights about the paintings he produced in retirement. (Painting was my home court and my instincts were sharper.) But I think he considered most of my architectural writing superficial, if slouching toward competence. Perhaps he was right.

By Hoosier standards his demeanor was, in a word, patrician. Yet he could be surprisingly open about himself. I think he would at least nod at this idea: heritage can be a surprising form of destiny.

Imagine the architect as a child, and the child as an architect. Imagine his father or perhaps his grandfather, both named Evans Woollen, telling the child, Evans Woollen III, born in 1927, how, a century before, his ancestor Samuel Merrill helped name the new state capital, a city imagined as a grid in the exact middle of the invisible statewide grid.

Almost two centuries later, Evans, now the best-known architect in the state, told his audience that architecture must mean more than the design of large, habitable structures. Rather, it must be understood and practiced as the choreography of perception and movement through space to create meaning. When spaces mean something to people they become places, and thus earn names.

In their times, both previous Evans Woollens were presidents of the Fletcher Trust Company (or descendants of that name), one of Indiana's major banks. Presumably this desk was waiting for the youngest Evans. But the boy decided to make buildings. Evans said he came to this decision (or it came to him) quite early, playing with wooden blocks in his sandbox. I imagine an afternoon later in the 1930s, the boy standing on the sidewalk just a half block east of Monument Circle, the center of the city, gazing up at his father's window in the bank tower, waving hello – or goodbye.

He once described himself as "the son and grandson of distinguished people I could never live up to. Having the same name puts a sort of curse on you." He asked, "Are you going to be up to those people? . . . If I was going to do it, I had to do it here [in Indianapolis]. I had an obligation here."

"Here" never meant more than it did for Evans. Born with a distinguished name at the heart of a distinguished family, a family at the heart of a city centered in its state and given its name. (A state "in the heart of the heart of the country," to quote William Gass.)

What's in a name? Here is one answer.

Steven Mannheimer is Emeritus Professor of Media Arts and Science at Indiana University Indianapolis. From 1982 to 2000 he was the visual arts writer for the *Indianapolis Star*.

What a Building Does

Intro-duc-tion

Indianapolis isn't known for its architecture; we're allowed to say this because we're from here. Corn, race cars, and conservative politics, plus a strange mixture of pride and insecurity in our hometown: these are our calling cards, if we have any at all. For many outsiders Indianapolis is easily stereotyped as "Indianoplace" – an average city in an average state, more readily defined by what it isn't rather than by what it is.

Evans Woollen thought differently. As a design-driven architect living and working in postwar Indianapolis, Woollen pointed to a richer identity for this city than was (and still is) usually imagined, one with a vitality and sense of place all its own. His output was vast and varied, spanning more than a half century of practice and multiple styles, typologies, and forms. And his buildings were often startlingly contemporary for their contexts, the handiwork of a shape-shifting architect adept at translating the field's most cutting-edge ideas for his own backyard.

Despite growing up in Indianapolis, we never knew Woollen's name. But we knew his buildings. Spend any time here and you're likely to stumble on a Woollen-designed library, church, school, theater, office, or house.

***Facing page*:**
Davlan Apartments, ca. 1972.
The building was refurbished by Woollen's firm and painted with its eye-catching corncob mural.

In the latter half of the twentieth century, few local architects were as prolific, even fewer in such ubiquitous fashion. "If there is one man mostly responsible for what Indianapolis looks like today, it would be the architect Evans Woollen," wrote the *Indianapolis Star* upon Woollen's death in 2016.[1]

In Hoosierland, Woollen's work resembled little else. His ambition was at turns visionary and obstinate, utopian and naive. "Controversial" was the descriptor often used by the city's press. Some loved his emphatic, proudly modern buildings. Others thought they were challenging, severe, even ugly. But Woollen's legacy is about far more than the divisiveness of his architecture. It also includes a multidecade practice of empathetic, human-centered design conducted long before such ideas were mainstream. "A building is what it does," he wrote in 1985, a six-word manifesto reiterated in the latter years of his career.[2] It was a reminder of what he saw to be architecture's true purpose: to enhance the lives of people through the places they inhabit.

This book aims to show what Woollen's buildings did. The ten projects featured here – a house, two theaters, a church, an apartment tower, an office building, a hotel, a library, and even a monastery – represent a cross section of Woollen's multifaceted portfolio. Drawing on new photography, never-before-seen archival material, and dozens of interviews with former colleagues, clients, and friends, we hope to give a sense of the ideas that shaped these buildings and contextualize their significance to the larger trajectory of modern architecture in the American Midwest.

In many ways Woollen's story is Indianapolis's story. His career coincided with the city's postwar regeneration, a period of unprecedented construction, destruction, and reimagination that thrust this once-sleepy frontier capital into the modern era. Although Woollen and his firm worked on projects across the country, we have chosen to focus here only on commissions in Indianapolis or a short drive away. Indianapolis was Woollen's home for most of his career, and although his relationship to it was sometimes tenuous, he claimed a special commitment to its flourishing.

As the first sustained look at Woollen's life, this book is by no means comprehensive. Much more can, and should, be said about him. Nonetheless, we hope it brings new awareness of this essential midwestern figure, illuminating the many meanings he designed into his architecture – and the new meanings we can glean from them today.

Indianapolis isn't known for its architecture. Maybe it should be?

Biog-raphy

TMY
TMY 5
TMY 4
TMY 3
TMY 2
KODAK TMY 6053
TMY 12
TMY 11
TMY 10
TMY 9
TMY 8
KODAK TMY 6053
KODAK TMY 6053
KODAK TMY 6053

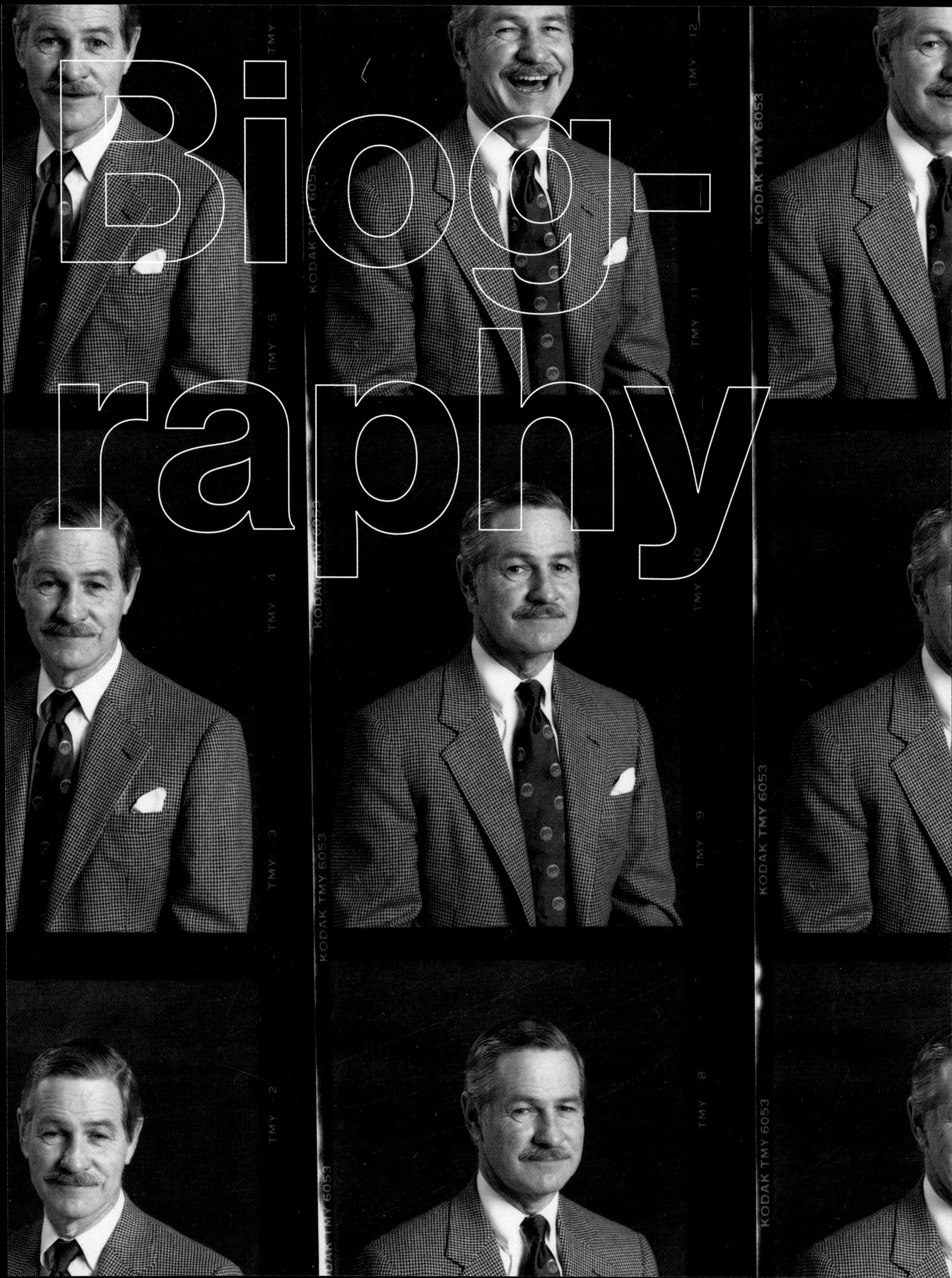

How to Be a Good Architect

Evans Woollen in Context

"This is the building that so many people love to hate," Evans Woollen announced.[1] Standing on stage in the darkened auditorium of the Indianapolis Museum of Art, Woollen looked more like a retired college professor than a controversy-courting architect, his silver hair and yellow bow tie suggesting an erudite sophistication as he spoke. The museum had invited the architect to deliver a lecture looking back on his long and variegated career, and Woollen – now in his 80s – appeared to be in a wistfully reflective mood. Projected behind him was a blurry snapshot of one of his most polarizing projects, the Minton-Capehart Federal Building, completed in 1974 – at the time of Woollen's talk in 2010, more than thirty years in the past. Those gathered to hear the architect speak that evening would have surely known it; the structure was one of the most recognizable in downtown Indianapolis. It was long and low, like a bunker, with a colorful abstract mural wrapped around its oblong base. Perhaps sensing a friendly audience, Woollen took the chance to correct the record. "I don't really want to defend it or change your ideas if you're set on hating it. That's ok. But I do welcome a chance to explain to open-minded listeners some of the factors that dictated the design of this building," he said.

Woollen was used to having to explain himself. Responsible for many of Indianapolis's most iconic, and iconoclastic, works of modern architecture, the designer had done more than most to shape the built environment of his hometown. His six-decade career of architectural creation had earned him the informal title of "dean of Indiana architects" – and, along with it, a reputation for provocation.[2] When it was all said and done, he wondered aloud that evening, what had led him here? "It was not fame, because I neglected the obvious paths to such," he told the audience.[3] "I didn't gravitate to New York City's metropolitan scene and join an avant-garde group, or become a stalwart adherent to a particular style. Please understand, this was – is – a commendable direction for anybody else. I just did not do it. Who knows why? There are no regrets."

***Facing page*:**
Picture day at Woollen, Molzan and Partners, ca. 1980s.

Woollen as a baby surrounded by his parents and grandparents.

Evans Woollen III was born on August 10, 1927, in Indianapolis. If his distinguished family tree was any indication, he was not destined to be an architect. He might have easily become a banker like his father or grandfather, Evans Woollen II and I, respectively, both prominent Indianapolis businessmen with local and national reputations. Or maybe a politician – his great-grandfather on his mother's side, Conrad Baker, had been the fifteenth governor of Indiana, and Evans I, too, had once run for president on the Democratic ticket. Or perhaps a lawyer, like his nineteenth-century ancestor Samuel Merrill, a leading citizen of the pioneer era and Indiana's second state treasurer. "How did I get into this family? What am I doing with these 'sober men folk'?" he mused to an interviewer near the end of his life.[4]

Woollen's father was a particularly intimidating figure. Known for his steely demeanor and three-piece suits, Evans II's name was synonymous with the family business, the Fletcher Savings and Trust Company, later known as the American Fletcher National Bank and Trust Company (after a series of mergers, the bank would be absorbed into Bank One, and then J. P. Morgan Chase). In 1948 the *Indianapolis News* described the banker in magisterial terms: "As he sits at his small mezzanine desk in the Fletcher Trust Co. he has three views. On his right is busy Market St. That's his town. Directly ahead of him are the top officers who help run the bank. And over his shoulder he can look into the well of the bank where faithful customers stream in and out, dealing with a banking family which has lived years and years in the strict confines of the Woollen principles."[5] An accompanying photo showed the entire Woollen family, including Woollen's mother, Lydia, and his two younger siblings, Jameson and Katharine.

By the time of Woollen's birth, his parents were firmly ensconced in Indianapolis's small but influential blue-blooded aristocracy. Patrons of many of the city's cultural institutions, they lived unusually cosmopolitan lifestyles for Indianapolis, and young Evans benefited from his parents' interest in art, music, and literature. Dan Wakefield, a family friend who would go on to vividly capture postwar Indianapolis in his novel *Going All the Way*, recounted once running into Mr. and Mrs. Woollen on a train traveling from Indianapolis to New York City. Over a spontaneous meal of steaks and whiskey sours in the dining car, the trio chatted about Broadway shows (a cultural offering not easily attained in provincial Indianapolis). The encounter gave Wakefield the "glorious feeling I was living a scene out of one of the novels of F. Scott Fitzgerald, my favorite author. The Woollens were the only people I knew in Indianapolis who might be in a Fitzgerald scene," as he later wrote.[6] The Woollens' affluence also meant their son received an education out of reach for most Hoosier children: boarding school at the elite Hotchkiss School in Lakeville, Connecticut, and then college at Yale University, his father and grandfather's alma mater.

"It sounds flippant, but I knew I wanted to be an architect when I was playing in the sand pile," Woollen once said.[7] Nonetheless, he would wrestle with the weight of his family's legacy for most of his life. His forebears had helped shape Indianapolis for decades, and the expectations set by their daunting achievements were hard to escape. No matter how different he hoped to be, in Indianapolis he would always be defined by his last name. "I didn't know how I could live up to it. And it took me a long time to realize that was ridiculous," he said.[8] Woollen would often recount the exact moment he asked his father permission to study architecture at Yale, a radical break in family tradition. Expecting pushback, instead he received something like a commandment: "He said to me very sternly, and it still rings in my ears, 'If you have to be an architect . . . you must be a good one.'"

His father would have little to worry about. An incubator for a generation of practitioners, Yale's architecture program would be an effective launch pad for Woollen as well. At Yale, architecture was no mere trade; it was the "art of building."[9] There Woollen immersed himself in a radically new approach to design, called modernism, which was revolutionizing architectural practice and would come to define Woollen's early career. Championed by European architects like Le Corbusier, Walter Gropius, and Ludwig Mies van der Rohe, modernism proclaimed rationalism, minimalism, and geometric purity as the design language of modern life. It was a stunning reversal from the ornate, historically inflected buildings Woollen had known from his childhood in Indianapolis, such as the Tudor Revival mansions he admired lining Meridian Street or the neoclassical John Herron Art Institute where his grandfather had been president of the board.[10] Yale brought him face-to-face with the architecture of the future: sleek and polished, rendered in glass, steel, and concrete – every element distilled to its most essentialized form.

At Yale, Woollen also made vital professional contacts that would steer his early trajectory. Faculty included some of the modern movement's preeminent practitioners, such as Edward Durrell Stone, Eliot Noyes, and the philosopher-architect Louis Kahn, a particularly influential figure for Woollen. Woollen's thesis jury included Kahn, the historian Henry-Russell Hitchcock, and Philip Johnson – one of the country's most famous (and mercurial) architects, and later Woollen's boss.[11] Johnson served as a proxy to the strict aesthetics of Miesian high modernism, also known as the International Style, and recently exemplified by Johnson's own residence in New Canaan, Connecticut, the Glass House. But it was Kahn who revealed the poetic, even spiritual possibilities that modern design could offer the world, a theme Woollen would later seize upon.
At some point during his studies Woollen also benefited from the mentorship of the architect Paul Schweikher, completing a summer internship in Schweikher's studio outside Chicago.[12] (Schweikher, coincidentally, would be named head of Yale's architecture program in 1953.)

Still, it was a time of transition, and at Yale the past remained very much present. The school was known for the "pluralism" of its curriculum, and a rotation of visiting critics exposed Woollen and his classmates to a diversity of viewpoints. In an era obsessed with the future, Woollen was especially taken by the architectural history classes taught by Yale historian Vincent Scully, whom he later called "the single strongest influence on me . . . although I would not have recognized it at the time" in a letter to the architect Robert A. M. Stern.[13] "Scully's passionate concern for American (as well as other) architects of different directions and periods did rub off rather permanently . . . allow[ing] me to become gradually detached from formal, personal, stylistic pressures in favor of social, programmatic and environmental issues as a basis for architecture," he continued. As Woollen shifted away from the dogma of high modernism in the second half of his career, such interests would assert themselves more strongly.

Because Yale's architecture program was then part of its art school, Woollen also benefited from a certain degree of interdisciplinary instruction. He studied drawing with the artist Josef Albers, who had joined Yale's faculty in 1950, and also took part in what was called the "collaborative problem," an annual studio project that brought together mixed teams of architecture, painting, and sculpture students to design a speculative building.[14] Woollen participated in "the problem's" 1948 edition, overseen by Kahn and the painter Jean Charlot.[15] Still an undergraduate, Woollen contributed not as an architect but as a sculptor. Kahn and Charlot must have been impressed by his team's results, and their highly futuristic design was one of six published by the magazine *Progressive Architecture* in April 1949.[16] The meaningful integration of art and architecture would be a central concern of Woollen's work to come.

Woollen stayed at Yale until 1952, completing both a bachelor's and a master's degree in architecture. He then spent three years working in New Canaan, Connecticut, a wealthy bedroom community about an hour's train ride from New York City. His Ivy League education had prepared him for architectural practice at the highest level. But it was New Canaan, then a hotbed of modern home design, that gave him his first taste of professional accomplishment. "It was a unique experience," Woollen later recounted to the critic Esther McCoy.[17] "John's [Johansen] greatest small house was under way, Philip Johnson was doing two or three very large houses, Eliot Noyes was building a house around the corner, and there were a number of others doing good work," he said. Apprenticing in Johnson's New Canaan–based studio before freelancing on his own, Woollen shrewdly attracted clients who wanted the International Style look – contemporary, elegant, refined – but could not afford an older or more experienced architect. To make ends meet, Woollen lived in a converted stable for fifty dollars a month.[18] In addition to his employment with Johnson, there is evidence that Woollen also

Naill house, 1954, a private residence designed by Woollen in New Canaan, Connecticut.

worked in some capacity for the architect Landis Gores, Johnson's former design partner, as well as for John Johansen, whom he met through Gores. The lengths of these stints are unknown.[19] (Woollen and Johansen would later collaborate on the Clowes Memorial Hall project in Indianapolis.)

Woollen's first commissions, all modest single-family homes in the New Canaan area with flat roofs and glass facades, demonstrated his inculcation in modernist purity. Here was Woollen at the nexus of American modern architecture, building buildings and rubbing shoulders with some of the most visionary practitioners of his day. By any measure a promising career at the very pinnacle of the profession stretched out before him. Woollen's decision then to relocate his practice – and his life – away from the East Coast and back to Indianapolis in 1955 may appear, in retrospect, surprising. For a young and ambitious architect operating within an elite environment of design innovation, what did Indianapolis have to offer him?

Over the years Woollen gave different reasons for why he chose to return home. One explanation was straightforward: he was in love. Nancy Clarke Sewell was born in Indianapolis but, like Woollen, went to school out East (in her case, Vassar College in Poughkeepsie, New York). As Woollen put it, Nancy "was firmly entrenched" in Indianapolis, so he needed to be too.[20] The two married in 1955 in the yard at Delaware Trail, the Woollen family homestead on the outskirts of the city.[21] The newlyweds soon moved into a sturdy brick home on Indianapolis's north side, but not before spending their honeymoon in one of Woollen's recently completed houses in New Canaan.[22]

There were also other, more nuanced motivations. After all, Woollen's local roots ran deep. His forebears had made Indianapolis their home for over a century, modeling a distinctly midwestern form of civic leadership and community altruism that Woollen could emulate. While previous Woollen men may have sought to improve their city through business or philanthropy, Woollen could make a difference – and therefore live up to the family name – in his own way: through architecture. (Even while he was a student at Yale, Indianapolis was never far from his mind. His thesis project was a design for a hypothetical combined campus for the Park School and Tudor Hall, two private schools back home.)[23] "I felt an obligation to help out," he explained to the *Indianapolis News* in 1962 in one of his first extended interviews with the paper.[24] "Indianapolis needs to keep a few sons at home – those with an appreciation of our historical past and an understanding of our yearnings for the future. I also came back because Indianapolis is a good-sized city that needs help in its growth. . . ." He then went on to declare just how fundamental Indianapolis was to his identity: "[Frank Lloyd] Wright was of the prairie and Eero Saarinen was of Detroit and the world of the auto. Indianapolis is my place." By invoking Wright and Saarinen, two of the biggest names in architecture at the time, Woollen was

Drawing for American Fletcher National Bank branch, 1957, Cumberland, Indiana.

making a bold pronouncement about the heights of his ambition—for both himself and for his city.

Although Woollen never mentioned it, there was also a clear business rationale for the move back home. In New Canaan, choosy clients could tap into a whole pool of architects, many of whom had graduated from the same top schools and adhered to the same design philosophies. Indianapolis, one could argue, was a far less competitive market. As an Ivy League graduate with real building experience, in Indianapolis Woollen would be a proverbial big fish in a small, midwestern pond. He could also lean on family connections. Some of Woollen's first Indianapolis projects were branch buildings for his father's bank, a helpful financial boost at the beginning of his career. Woollen completed no fewer than four branch designs, as well as an interior renovation of the bank's downtown headquarters.[25]

***Above*:**
Fesler Hall, a classroom building on the campus of the Herron School of Art, 1962.

***Below*:**
Headquarters building for the Indiana Credit Union League, 1964.

Woollen's father died suddenly in 1959, never seeing the heights of his son's success. Woollen's firm, soon named Woollen Associates, was on its way to becoming one of if not the leading architectural practice in the city. It was at least the most exciting, regarded for its daring (and frequently divisive) designs. In the 1960s and 1970s Woollen and his firm worked on a wide variety of project typologies: a community center, a library, a hotel, a church, a school, a concert hall, an apartment tower, a neighborhood master plan. Many of these commissions were in and around central Indiana, a remarkable concentration of built work by a single architect. Bold and geometric, typically wrought in concrete, brick, or glass, these buildings expressed an avant-garde vision of contemporary life which, in twentieth-century Indianapolis, stood out from the norm. While locally unusual, they in fact reflected their designer's awareness of and engagement with the cutting edge of national and international architectural discourse. Many of the era's

Marian University library, 1970.

major architectural trends – International Style modernism, concrete Brutalism, murals and supergraphics, and postmodern classicism among them – found root in Woollen's work, resynthesized and contextualized for the context at hand. In this way Woollen served as one of the city's most visible champions for a more ambitious architectural identity, as well as a pacesetter for his local peers.

Woollen was by no means the only modern architect working in Indianapolis during this era. However, his Ivy League training, flair for boundary-pushing design, and ability to garner local and national press coverage put him in a class of his own. A parade of newspaper profiles and magazine articles reliably heralded Woollen's success. "Physically, Evans Woollen III is a space saver – just a little man. Architecturally, he's a giant with national recognition," the *Indianapolis News* told its readers in 1967, one of several laudatory stories the paper and its main competitor, the *Indianapolis Star*, published over the years.[26] The firm frequently showed up in the pages of prestigious national architectural magazines – a feat for any small regional studio – where it was cited by important critics like McCoy and Sibyl Moholy-Nagy. From 1955 to 1990, the firm's work received article-length treatment at least eighteen times in either *Architectural Forum* or *Architectural Record* (two of which were cover stories), along with numerous other mentions in publications like *Progressive Architecture*, *Arts & Architecture*, and *Zodiac: International Magazine of Contemporary Architecture*.[27] Texts were usually accompanied by cinematic images from Balthazar Korab, Woollen's photographer of choice, or renderings by the virtuosic architectural illustrator Helmut Jacoby.

STAR MAGAZINE

Indianapolis May 9, 1976 SUNDAY

EVANS WOOLLEN: Struggles Of A 'Good' Architect Page 18

Woollen on the cover of *Indianapolis Star Magazine*, May 9, 1976.

For the discerning readers of the national trade magazines, Woollen was a bold and dynamic modern architect, but something of a novelty – a Johnson acolyte making his way "out there" in the midwestern hinterlands. In Indianapolis his reputation was far more mixed. His buildings stood out, their bombastic use of material, color, and form testing the aesthetic preferences of a generally conservative populace. Not everyone was a fan. "The most accomplished, controversial and avant garde architect in Indianapolis is not the most popular man in town," read the first line of a splashy cover story on Woollen published by the *Indianapolis Star Magazine* in 1976.[28] Woollen – never at a loss for words – shot back: "An architect can't be effective if he isn't controversial," he said in the same article.[29]

Soon the firm grew to fifteen, then twenty, then twenty-five. The influx of work in Indiana and, increasingly, beyond meant that Woollen had to be both architect and manager of a growing business. Lynn Molzan, a graduate of the Pratt Institute who had joined the practice in 1965, would become instrumental to the firm's growing success and handle most operational matters. "Lynn was a perfect foil to Evans. While Evans would be eccentric and all about ideas and sort of really off in his own world, Lynn brought reality to it, and managed the people that needed to support creating these visions," said Kevin Huse, another longtime leader in the firm.[30] Fittingly, the business was renamed Woollen, Molzan and Partners in 1982. By all accounts Woollen and Molzan worked well together. But no matter how large the firm became, Woollen remained the last word on all things design. "He was a one-man marketing and design visionary," observed architect Deborah A. Burkhart, who worked for the firm in the 1980s before becoming a principal at Ross Barney Architects in Chicago.[31] "All the other partners [in the firm] were there to support him. He was the starchitect of Indianapolis, maybe the state," she said.

Woollen ran the studio as an architectural atelier with a level of discipline and formality he had likely absorbed at Yale. "At other firms, there's a little more chatter. Radios are playing in the background. But Woollen had serious people – and that came down from him," remembered Laurence O'Connor, a partner in the firm for much of its existence.[32] Nonetheless, a certain level of egalitarianism in the design process was permissible within the studio's hierarchy. Senior architects were given real ownership over individual projects, and even junior staff were able to bring new ideas to the table. Pinups gave the whole studio a chance to weigh in on a project's direction. That didn't mean Woollen treated anyone with kid gloves; his criticism was always direct, and often biting. "He suffered no fools, but he was not the type that made a sketch on a napkin and simply tossed it off and said, 'Make something like this.' He was collaborative," said James McQuiston, a staff architect during the 1970s who went on to launch his own practice in the city.[33]

A. J. Thatcher Community Center, 1973.

***Above*:**
Unidentified house design.

***Right*:**
Pruis Hall at Ball State University, 1972.

For employees and clients alike, it was also inescapable that Woollen was of a certain social class. His famous ancestry and old-school, relationship-based approach to business gave the firm access to the city's power brokers, a sort of secret weapon that the firm leveraged to win new work. "Today, you can't rely on the identity of the architect alone. You've got to get a marketing department. Evans came from another world. To him, marketing meant going to the country club Christmas party," observed Steve Mannheimer, who got to know the architect over the years as the arts writer for the *Indianapolis Star*.[34] With his sharp tailoring and penchant for bow ties, Woollen certainly looked the part of the East Coast aesthete (especially when tooling around town in his diesel Mercedes), and accusations of elitism – a cardinal sin for meritocratic, salt-of-the-earth Hoosiers – dogged him for most of his career. Yet few could argue with his intellect and unabashed passion for the work. Staff members often marveled at their boss's ability to sell clients on even the most unusual idea. "He was the most articulate person. He would have made a great lawyer," recalled Peter Mayer, a junior architect whom Woollen recruited directly from Yale in the 1960s.[35] Woollen often entertained the staff at his own home, an old Tudor Revival that had once been the childhood home of author Kurt Vonnegut. "Evans kind of had a salon going at his house," recalled Graham Greene, a staff architect who joined several of these gatherings and would go on to lead the Dallas firm Oglesby Greene Architecture.[36] "In his backyard was a constant flow of people – artisans, politicians, students. It was quite a mix, a kind of a cross section of the arts and culture community in Indianapolis at the time." And at the center of it all was Woollen, a willing sparring partner in debates on architecture, art, theory, politics, and more.

Intellectually vibrant and culturally rich, Woollen's "salons" projected an aspirational picture of what life in Indianapolis was like.

***Above*:**
Aerial view of downtown Indianapolis, 1968.

***Below*:**
Woollen Associates office, identifiable by the giant 7UP sign on its roof, in downtown Indianapolis.

The reality, however, was far different. "Indianapolis as an urban place was pretty dreadful. It just wasn't an exciting place to be. A big night in 1975 was to go to TGIFridays in the suburbs," remembered staff architect Alan Weiskopf, who would later head the firm Perfido Weiskopf Wagstaff + Goettel in Pittsburgh.[37] Such problems were hardly new. Years of disinvestment had left basic urban infrastructure to crumble, leaving large swaths of the downtown area blighted and in decline. New highways threatened to dice up the city's core and displace thousands, while "white flight" put increasing emphasis on suburban living. It was a familiar story unfolding in cities across the country during the postwar era, leading local and national observers to wonder whether urbanism's days were numbered. "Is the city doomed?" asked the *Indianapolis Star Magazine* in 1953.[38]

Woollen disagreed. Influenced by pro-city, pro-density urbanists like Jane Jacobs, Woollen served as a passionate advocate for downtown Indianapolis and its long-term vitality. And as Indianapolis embarked on an ambitious series of capital investments and urban renewal projects in the latter half of the twentieth century, he believed architects and urban planners – not just politicians and developers – were essential to any decision-making about the city's trajectory. Appearing once at a planning commission hearing for a proposed high-rise development outside the city core, Woollen launched in: "Give us density where we so desperately need it; save our low density where it best thrives at a distance from the heart. Let us have planning by consensus not by greed," he said.[39] Woollen's outspokenness was not always welcome. A rare Democrat in a Republican-run city, his politics (and razor-sharp tongue) sometimes put him at odds with the powers that be. Yet there could be little doubt about Woollen's genuine care for his hometown. "He's the most stubborn s.o.b. I've ever known. But he's a magnificent citizen," an anonymous local philanthropist told the *Indianapolis Star Magazine*.[40]

One of Woollen's most frequent complaints related to what he called the "pioneer attitude" of his fellow Hoosiers – a nagging, ingrained propensity to look outside the state for solutions that might just as well be found in their own backyard.[41] "The ethos, or characteristic spirit, of this city is made up by too many people who would rather be somewhere else. They engender an inferiority complex hard to overcome by those who would love this place," he told an interviewer plainly in 1963.[42] Such comments were no doubt colored by his own complex relationship with the city of his birth. Woollen had found considerable success in Indianapolis, and his local reputation loomed large. Still, he felt stymied by the ceiling placed on his ambition – forever the local son defined not by what he could do, but by where he was from.

"This is the hardest, most difficult place to be recognized," he complained openly to the *Indianapolis Star Magazine* in his 1976 cover story, an ironic statement given the large amount of press his work was receiving from both local and national outlets during this

Woollen with Hotchkiss School students. He served as campus architect for the school, his alma mater, during the 1970s.

period, arguably the apogee of his career.[43] Nonetheless, it was this paradox that led him to open a short-lived satellite office in Boston in 1987, and then to take a leave of absence from his firm – and his city – entirely. If Indianapolis was stifling, perhaps the notoriety and professional opportunity he sought could be found back on the East Coast where he had begun his career. In 1989 he joined Boston's Payette Associates, a much larger practice with more high-profile projects, as a principal. It was an odd arrangement that ended up being only temporary; Woollen returned home from his "sabbatical" after two years. "I was feeling a need to be in a different world for a while, if only to see this world a little better," he later explained.[44]

Although Woollen's frustrations were clearly personal, they were certainly rooted in a degree of truth. More than once in Indiana's history had enterprising Hoosiers turned to more famous, out-of-town architects as a means of burnishing the cultural profile of their communities. In the 1950s businessmen Joseph Cantor and Harry Berke tapped Mies van der Rohe to design a series of public and private projects across Indianapolis. In the 1960s the town of Fort Wayne, Indiana, hired Kahn (after approaching Mies, Johnson, and Saarinen) to develop a new arts complex. In the 1970s Indiana University Bloomington commissioned I. M. Pei for a campus art museum (a job Woollen also vied for, unsuccessfully), and in the 1980s Indianapolis civic leaders engaged César Pelli to design Indiana Tower, a 750-foot-tall architectural folly intended as a new landmark for the state on the scale of the St. Louis Gateway Arch or Chartres Cathedral.[45] Only rarely did Hoosier budgets match the scope of Hoosier ambitions and, as a result, few of these projects came to fruition as planned.

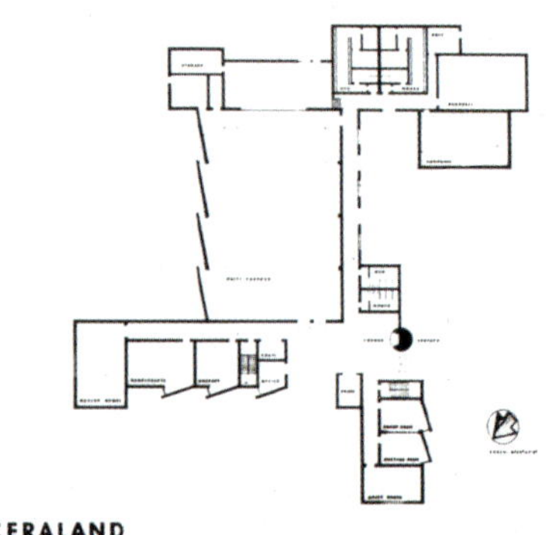

***Above*:**
Model for Woollen's Cummins Employee Recreation Association building, late 1960s.

***Below*:**
Floorplan for Woollen's Cummins Employee Recreation Association building, late 1960s.

The strongest example of this "pioneer attitude" was also likely the most difficult for Woollen to ignore. Its epicenter could be found just forty miles south of Indianapolis in Columbus, Indiana, a small farming community along the White River whose architectural identity was systematically transformed over several decades thanks to the efforts of one local businessman, J. Irwin Miller. As CEO of the Cummins Engine Company, Columbus's largest business and primary employer, Miller rightly understood the power of celebrity architects to elevate his hometown. "You can't pioneer any more by hacking out new land. But you can through architecture," he told *Time* magazine in 1977.[46] Either acting on his own or working under the aegis of his company's philanthropic arm, the Cummins Engine Foundation, and its dedicated architecture program, Miller coaxed a carefully curated list of blue-chip architects – Saarinen, Johansen, Pei, Pelli, Kevin Roche, Richard Meier, and many others – to design buildings in Columbus.[47] Virtually all these architects were from outside the state.[48] Miller's architectural world-building also extended to Indianapolis, where he was similarly responsible for the architectural pedigree of major projects like Irwin Library at Butler University, designed by Minoru Yamasaki, and the Christian Theological Seminary, designed by Edward Larrabee Barnes.

Woollen was arguably the most distinguished architect practicing in Indiana at the time of Miller's building spree, yet he remained conspicuously disconnected from Miller's patronage and the Columbus project as a whole. Little is known of the two men's relationship (if one even existed at all), but it is hard to imagine that Miller was not at least familiar with Woollen's work. The two certainly shared much in common: both descended from prominent Indiana families, were Yale graduates, and believed deeply in the power of architecture to transform a community. They may have crossed paths socially: Miller's wife, Xenia, served alongside Nancy Woollen for a time on the board of the Indianapolis Theological Seminary, and his aunt, Elsie Irwin Sweeney, was a major donor to Indiana University's Musical Arts Center designed by Woollen.[49] There is also evidence that Woollen's firm did in fact work on a project in Columbus sometime in the late 1960s. Little documented and virtually unknown today, the project – a fitness center for the Cummins Employee Recreation Association – does not appear to have been officially part of the Cummins Foundation architecture program, and Miller's actual involvement in the commission is unclear.[50] Due to an unrelated employee strike, the project never made it past the design phase. (Harold Roth eventually designed a new rec center for the association in 1982.)

Whatever the circumstances, a Miller commission – and the prestige that would have accompanied it – remains a noticeable omission on Woollen's résumé. According to outside observers, it was an oversight that likely stung. Woollen rarely spoke publicly about Miller, only telling the *Indianapolis Star Magazine* in 1974 that he would be

***Above*:**
Over-the-Rhine, 1975. The project consisted of a neighborhood master plan and four new buildings. Distinctive supergraphics identified the new among the old.

***Right*:**
Planning meeting for Over-the-Rhine held in the firm's pop-up studio. Woollen is seated at right against the wall.

"honored" to work for the businessman if asked.[51] Nonetheless, he was known to gripe at the larger cultural biases at play. "Certainly it's good to have outside practitioners come in and set high standards. But it's bad when this becomes all pervasive. Moreover, it demonstrates veiled feelings of inferiority. If you have to import everything, you can't feel too good about yourself," he opined in 1982.[52]

Whether coincidentally or not, by the late 1970s and 1980s Woollen's architecture was evolving. Previously he had aspired to be the Frank Lloyd Wright of Indianapolis, to create architecture that would make an unforgettable statement on behalf of both him and his city. Now his goals were becoming much more subdued, a corrective to the "many decades in the past of architects beating their breasts about their artistic insights and prowess," he said.[53] No longer interested in the brash, avant-garde monuments for which he had earned his reputation, he began to favor an architecture that was far quieter and unafraid of history or precedent. "People don't like having statements made to them. They'd rather be whispered to," he said in 1988.[54] Futuristic glass boxes were jettisoned for familiar vernacular elements like pitched roofs and dormers. Cold concrete gave way to warmer plaster and wood. Woollen was by no means alone in this change. Propelled by Robert Venturi's theory of "complexity and contradiction" in architecture, the entire field was drifting toward a new paradigm, called postmodernism, which favored historicism, decoration, and even whimsy over the cool rationalism of modernist design.[55] Woollen admired the work of leading postmodernists like Venturi and Charles Moore, and the firm's output from this period clearly bears their influence.[56]

Woollen, ca. 1980s.

However, for Woollen there may have been a deeper undercurrent to this shift. Woollen had been schooled in the tradition of the architect as "form giver" – that architecture was synonymous with making new marks on the earth. But as his career progressed, he began to believe in an evolved form of practice that was less about him and more about the world. Contextualism, guided by a respect for the spatial and social environments which surrounded any building, became his primary concern. "I was more and more conscious that the most important thing an architect could do was to collaborate with the physical environment rather than contrast with it," he explained.[57] While some saw this change as merely stylistic, another aesthetic about-face in a practice that had often flitted from one design trend to the next, others recognized a greater meaning. "I personally never thought of the work as postmodern. It was about community. It was about something that builds on what many people have worked on before, and will continue to work on after," remembered architect Kalevi Huotilainen, a leader in the firm during this period. "In my mind, Evans had two eras: his modernist era and his contextual era. I was very proud to be a part of the second era," he said.[58]

Master planning work offered Woollen the chance to explore an integrated architecture beyond the single building. The firm completed a number of planning projects over the years, including for the Union Station area in downtown Indianapolis; a cultural district in South Bend, Indiana, called Michiana Place; and an ill-fated scheme for a large public park in Richmond, Indiana, codeveloped with the Californian artist James Turrell. One of his most innovative planning projects was for Over-the-Rhine, a racially diverse neighborhood in Cincinnati with a significant number of historic nineteenth-century structures. While other architects may have elected to raze the entire area and start fresh, Woollen took a far more empathic approach. Influenced by participatory design pioneers William Caudill and David Lewis, Woollen's firm opened a storefront office in an

***Below*:**
Unbuilt proposal for a judicial court building in downtown Indianapolis, 1987.

***Right*:**
Indianapolis Public School no. 47, 1982.

old butcher shop and engaged community members on their own turf. This local input was reflected in the final plan, which surgically inserted new buildings between and around existing structures without disrupting the area's historic fabric. In 1975 *Architectural Record* featured the project on its October cover, lauding the firm for its unusually sensitive approach to urban infill.[59]

Over-the-Rhine set the tone for many projects to come, particularly for educational clients like schools and libraries where charrettes, workshops, and community interviews became essential ingredients in the design process. Woollen called this philosophy "situational architecture," a way of thinking about practice that was outside in rather than inside out; that saw the architect as an orchestrator of stakeholders rather than an arbiter of taste; and that considered finished buildings merely as suspended moments in an ongoing continuum of change. In 1985 Woollen summarized his thinking in an essay for *Arts & Architecture* titled "Towards an Architecture of Process." The piece was a full-throated appeal to architectural humanism, calling for "less an architecture of Le Corbusier's machines, more an architecture modeled on organisms, or for that matter, modeled on life."[60] Citing Carl Jung, Lao Tsu, and the philosopher Alfred North Whitehead, the essay confirmed just how poetic – even mystical – Woollen's ideas about architecture had become.[61] "Individual buildings may be non beings unless they work together with others to make a wheel. In its tangible life on earth, architecture gains meaning when it relates to the surrounding people, their past, their environment, both natural and physical, the genius loci," he wrote.

By the 1990s Woollen, Molzan and Partners was predominantly occupied with higher education projects outside Indiana. These buildings, many of them libraries, extended the firm's enchantment with context-driven design. Woollen, pushing seventy, had largely stepped back from the firm's daily operations. In 1993 he was elected to the College of Fellows of the American Institute of Architects, one of the field's highest achievements. A short documentary broadcast on Indianapolis public television feted his career. Then came the most important commission of his professional life: a landmark, $82 million expansion to the Indianapolis Public Library's flagship branch. In the twilight of his career, the project was Woollen's last chance to leave a legacy in the city of his birth. What should have been a victory lap turned out to be an albatross: as construction got underway, the building's foundation became mired in structure deficiencies, resulting in massive budget overruns and a raft of lawsuits. Although the finished library was ultimately hailed as a success – and Woollen, Molzan and Partners cleared of any wrongdoing – the very public controversy left a mark. The firm quietly folded in 2011.

Despite once claiming "I would like to die with my boots on," Woollen more or less retired from architecture.[62] There was a sense

Woollen house, 2003.

of finality to the decision. He gave away his architecture books and moved out of the city, seeking to close one chapter of his life and open a new one. "His heart was still about being creative, but he wanted to explore his creative and even spiritual side through other things," remembered Ted Halsey, a former mentee at the firm who spent time with him during this later period.[63] Painting and watercolors, passions Woollen had explored as a resident at the American Academy in Rome in 1997, became his primary artistic pursuit. His work leaned toward abstraction, favoring euclidean geometries set on planes of solid color. The meanings of these compositions were usually left unsaid, although Woollen's naming sometimes provided a hint. He titled one large painting, an architectural arrangement of squares, circles, and triangles, simply "After Louis Kahn."

For the first time in his life Woollen moved into a home of his own design, a modest artists' retreat located on fifteen remote acres outside Boulder, Colorado. Dusty pink with electric blue trellises, the spartan home would not have appealed to everyone, but perhaps that was the point. In the open living room Woollen hung one of his largest paintings opposite three massive south-facing windows that flooded the room with mountain light. After a half century of building for others, the architect had finally created something for himself.

What is Woollen's legacy today? It is a question not so easily answered. His work conformed to no single style, trend, or dogma. At various times he was a minimalist, a maximalist, an individualist, a regionalist, a contextualist. Sometimes he created forms that embraced the future; at other times, the past. Toward Indianapolis he played cheerleader and critic in equal measure, a proud "local architect" – and anything but. These paradoxes are part of his story. But above all, Woollen was a humanist. He designed for people. Whether a single-family home or an entire city, he believed in architecture as a deeply empathic endeavor, one that – when perfectly calibrated – might yield work of enduring social resonance. Buildings were more than immutable dots on a flat midwestern landscape. They were also backdrops for the richness of communal life. And most

Woollen's last commission, one of three private homes in suburban Indianapolis, 2008.

importantly, their meaning accrued in layers, becoming fully realized only after generations of use. "Music takes time to experience its full impact, but architecture, I would argue, takes much more time," Woollen told his audience that evening in 2010 at the Indianapolis Museum of Art.[64] "There can be a factor of slow release. Sometimes a building is despised at the beginning and beloved at the end – or the reverse, it must be admitted. I will abide by the end myself."

Woollen died on May 17, 2016. Before his passing he completed one final commission: a trio of private homes sited on a rare plot of undeveloped land at the edge of Indianapolis city limits. His clients had interviewed several architects in town, only to discover that everyone interesting had once worked at Woollen, Molzan and Partners. So why not go after the real thing? After successfully luring Woollen out of retirement, they gave him something he rarely received: creative freedom. As could be expected, the design process was anything but transactional. Woollen even insisted his clients make a pilgrimage to his home in Colorado so they could get to know their architect in his own environment.

The three houses Woollen ultimately delivered were each unique in their own ways, custom-built for their occupants' habits and behaviors based on careful study. But they were also all distinctively Woollen. His hand was evident in their clean-cut profiles, intuitive massing, and light-filled interiors. Composed but warm, rational but painterly, they represented a lifetime of architectural thinking.

Proj-
ects

Parke House
Clowes Memorial Hall
Barton Tower
St. Thomas Aquinas Church
Musical Arts Center
Minton-Capehart Federal Building
New Harmony Inn
Saint Meinrad Monastery
Children's Museum of Indianapolis
Central Library

Parke House

Parke house, 1955.

Thomas V. Parke House

1955 | Indianapolis, IN

The house on Indianapolis's rural northeast side wasn't large, but it certainly was memorable. Built out of concrete, steel, and glass, the dwelling was akin to a two-story shoebox, painted stark white and nestled on a sloping wooded site. Its roof was flat and cantilevered, jutting out over the home's unadorned facades like a lid slightly too big for its receptacle. For the first time visitor there was no obvious front or back – just form and color, a crisp mirage of geometric shape peeking through the site's dense foliage.

Inside, it didn't feel like a house either, or at least not the sort one was likely to encounter in suburban Indianapolis. Like the exterior, most interior walls were made of exposed concrete block, while floors were covered in a slick terrazzo. The plan's defining feature was a vast great room measuring fifty feet long and sixteen feet high, and dominated by edge-to-edge windows that overlooked a fern-covered ravine. The home's physical and metaphorical center, all other rooms – a kitchen and study on the first floor, and three small bedrooms on the second – fed into this large, columnless space.

The result was an unusually open and interconnected living environment whose character seemed to transform with the passing of the sun – bright and airy during the day, moody at night. The liberal use of glass gave the distinct impression of living in a fishbowl, or maybe a terrarium (the interior temperature was notoriously difficult to regulate, and the glass panes were always susceptible to condensation). Emphasizing transparency at every turn, enclosures were kept to a minimum; for instance, the second floor bedrooms were accessible by an exposed spiral staircase and then an open catwalk that overlooked the great room and the vista beyond.

The home was designed for Eli Lilly chemist Thomas V. Parke and completed in 1955, making it likely Woollen's first built work in Indianapolis following his return to the city from New Canaan, Connecticut. It was an auspicious beginning: two years later, *Architectural Record* named the project a "Record House," a prestigious title doled out annually to the year's most innovative domestic designs. *Record* noted the house's "big room concept" – unusual for the time – and use of cost-effective, prefabricated elements.[1] Woollen, the only Indiana architect included that year, was in good company: Eliot Noyes's own residence in New Canaan (now known as the Noyes House II) was also cited, as well as homes by other established practitioners like Philip Johnson and Walter Gropius's Architects Collaborative. Virtually every one was a variation on the same rectilinear modernist theme. For Woollen, the award was decisive proof that national acclaim would be still be possible even in a secondary market like Indianapolis. The Parke house was also featured later that year in the Sunday *New York Times* alongside three other Record Houses, all "in the modern mode."[2]

The Parke house (also known as the Edelson or Zazas residence after subsequent owners) epitomized the types of projects on which Woollen would initially stake his career: simple, budget-friendly homes strongly influenced by the modernist principles he had absorbed during his formative years in New Haven and New Canaan. While visually striking, these early works mirrored larger nationwide trends in postwar domestic living that went far beyond aesthetics alone. The years following World War II were a period of profound transformation for American society, a shift catalyzed by the return of thousands of GIs from the warfront. A postwar economic boom coupled with new technological possibilities portended a rapid modernization of public and private life. Homeownership exploded. And home design, especially in the country's growing suburban areas, began to reflect a new domestic ideal, one that was less rigid and more expansive than had previously been the norm.[3]

The Parke house exemplified such changes, demonstrating modernism's true aim as not only a style of architecture but as an all-encompassing mode of living. Formal sitting rooms and servants' quarters of the past were replaced by open, flexible spaces that often combined living and dining functions. Light was a principal concern ("I myself am a glutton for light, always raising shades and pushing curtains aside wherever I go. A very annoying guest, I am like a plant," Woollen once remarked).[4] Sliding doors and patios encouraged indoor-outdoor entertaining, while exposed staircases and "mezzanine" floors with interior balconies embraced a new lifestyle of transparency and informality.[5]

It was an architecture for a nation in transition, personified by the upwardly mobile homeowner searching for his or her own version of the American Dream. "The new architecture is a frontier architecture, an architecture built as much to move out of as to move into," wrote the cultural observer Russell Lynes in the same issue of *Record* that included the Parke house. "The American house has become a stepping-stone. It has become a stop on an incessant journey. Indeed, some of the houses in this issue of the *Record* seem to be in motion themselves, hovering just above the ground, not on it, as though they might flap their wings and migrate at any moment."[6]

The Parke house was a remarkably pure distillation of modernist conventions, built by a young architect who had yet to develop his own identifiable approach. It repurposed a template Woollen had already used in New Canaan on a two-bedroom home for *New York Herald Tribune* cartoonist Paul Arlt. One of at least three homes Woollen designed in the area during his time there, the commission came to him via the architect John Johansen who deemed the project's design fees too low for himself to take on and instead recommended Woollen to the client.[7] Photographs of the original structure (the home has since been significantly altered) show a modest, glass-fronted rectangle dramatically perched on a concrete block base in the Connecticut woods. The symmetrical floor plan was similar to the Parke house, consisting of a combination living- and dining "big room" flanked by a bedroom and kitchen on one side and a study and secondary bedroom on the other. All structural elements were plainly visible, with equal horizontal and vertical sections milled from the same lumber. "The objective was order . . . however superficial," Woollen later remembered of the design, an impulse he attributed directly to Johansen's influence.[8] A few years later, the Arlt house would be part of a New Canaan home tour which also included Johnson's famed Glass House and other modern masterpieces of this period.[9]

Arlt house, 1954, New Canaan, Connecticut. © The estate of Pedro E. Guerrero.

In New Canaan, Woollen's glass box fit right in. But in 1950s Indianapolis such avant-garde architectural expressions were exceedingly unconventional. Transitioning to Indianapolis, Woollen later remembered, was "like being parachuted into a different climate. It was very rough," and he initially struggled to find work.[10] Broadly, midcentury Indianapolis was dominated by two types of residential design languages: historic revival styles – Victorian, Tudor, Italianate, Colonial – so popular among homebuilders and buyers in the previous decades, and newer (and cheaper) ranch types, which, by the 1940s and 1950s, were proliferating in exurban areas.[11] By comparison, "contemporary" styles (as they were often called at the time) were relatively rarer, more readily found in the pages of glossy shelter magazines like *House Beautiful* or *House & Garden* than in the city's neighborhoods. In addition to Woollen, only a handful of local practitioners – Edward D. Pierre, Harry Cooler, Howard Wolner, and the self-trained designer Avriel Shull among them – were committed to modernism in domestic architecture, and even within this tiny coterie, Woollen's work could be seen as particularly rigorous and uncompromising.[12] While compatriots like Shull favored the warm romanticism of Frank Lloyd Wright's Prairie Style, Woollen was more firmly aligned with the International Style severity of Johnson and Mies van der Rohe. (Interestingly, Woollen did experiment with the Prairie Style during his time at Yale – his very first built work, a vacation cottage for a Yale professor completed while he was still in college, was clearly Wrightian – but he did not continue these explorations in professional practice.)

Even if Indianapolis did not have the same concentration of modern houses as New Canaan or, say, Chicago (then also a locus for modern home design), modern domestic architecture was by no means completely unknown. Locals may have gotten their first close look at home design's next wave in their own city as early as 1933 – not in the form of constructed buildings but via photographs and models displayed in a pivotal exhibition at the John Herron Art Institute. The "International Exhibition of Modern Architecture" was a traveling version of an earlier exhibition organized by Johnson and Henry-Russell Hitchcock (both later to be Woollen's thesis jurors at Yale) for New York's Museum of Modern Art. The MoMA presentation had done much to popularize the work of modern architects like Wright, Mies, and Le Corbusier for American audiences, and it likely had the same effect in Indianapolis.[13] There visitors would have encountered now seminal works like Fallingwater, Wright's dramatically cantilevered residence in southern Pennsylvania, alongside other examples of modern domestic design by Walter Gropius, Marcel Breuer, and Johnson himself. (While Herron did not have a strong focus on architecture, the museum would exhibit the work of Eliel and Eero Saarinen in 1942, and Breuer in 1950.)

Unlike the artistically driven creations presented at Herron, the first modern homes actually erected in Indianapolis were likely designed as spec homes by private developers who, by the late 1930s, were working to spark an interest in contemporary styles and new fabrication techniques among the public. In 1937 the H. L. Horton Company constructed a streamlined three-bedroom "house of tomorrow" made out of concrete masonry block and finished with white stucco and metal trim. The house, which still stands in Indianapolis's Broad Ripple neighborhood, was described by the *Indianapolis Star* as "unusual in its modernistic theme" and "a machine for living" (this last phrase a quotation from Corbusier, although the paper did not cite him).[14] A similar strategy was followed by the American Dwellings Co., led by former Purdue University researcher Frank Watson, which constructed at least four starkly minimalist spec homes out of prefabricated plywood in the city. "The most compact, completely modern dwelling ever offered to Indianapolis home-buyers," claimed one advertisement for the company's "House No. 2," built on Keystone Avenue.[15] Watson's work was soon featured in the pages of *Architectural Forum,* which noted the radicality of his company's experiments. "The most significant fact, perhaps, to emerge from the experience with this house, 1957 is that the buying public is by no means as hostile to modern as lending agencies apparently believe. Of the 12,000 who have visited the house, less than 10 per cent objected to the appearance of the exterior or the interior," the magazine claimed.[16]

For those interested, modernism was also on hand at the Indianapolis Home Show, a nationally known showcase of home design trends and an important barometer of changing tastes in domestic architecture. In 1933 the show's popular model home competition featured, for the very first time, an "ultramodern" spec house with a flat roof and silver trim. Its futuristic styling caused something of a scandal, and competition organizers would not

Hughes House, 1957.

veer from more traditional vernaculars for several years.[17] By the 1950s, modernism was featured somewhat more regularly, but still remained outside the norm. The 1958 competition featured, unusually, two winners: a contemporary home, with wide overhangs and a glass front; and a Colonial "period" home, with quaint dormer windows and a white picket fence. While the period home was conceived for broad appeal, the contemporary home was, according to one report, "definitely not designed for the average family and is not meant to fulfill the needs of every viewer."[18]

Within this environment, Woollen slowly began to attract clients – generally budget-conscious young families who were intrigued by the futuristic forms the architect was creating. Usually constructed simply with inexpensive or off-the-shelf materials, the prototypical modernist design offered savings over traditional styles. Woollen's ability to deliver cutting-edge aesthetics at an accessible price point became something of a signature, a strategy purpose-built for the postwar homeowner. James and Sheila Hughes fit this description. Inspired by the contemporary architecture they had encountered while living on the East Coast, the design-minded couple was determined to find a similar house when they moved to Indianapolis to start a family. The Woollen-designed home they purchased in 1967 from its original owner was the opposite of the traditional style of houses they had each grown up in, but it was exactly what they were looking for.

Delta Zeta sorority house, 1960.

Originally built for less than $20,000, the Hugheses' new home had been previously featured in *House & Garden* as an example of modernism on a budget. "Its type of classic, rectilinear design is often used for houses of more imposing proportions and cost. Yet the architect, working within the very modest budget, incorporated such uncommon features as 10' ceilings, covered decks on two sides of the house, a hall skylight, custom cabinets, recessed lighting fixtures, and large expanses of glass," the magazine reported.[19] For the Hugheses and their daughter, Meghan, Woollen's creation was like living in a movie. "I didn't have a single friend with a house that looked anything like it. People loved it. You felt special in that house. To have something that beautiful and different and not be a multi-millionaire, it felt exotic and special," recalled Meghan.[20] The family lived in the home for thirty-five years, forging a personal relationship with Woollen.

In 1960 Woollen applied these same principles on a larger scale when he completed a seventy-two-bed sorority house for the Delta Zeta sorority at DePauw University in Greencastle, Indiana. Now demolished, the three-story, rectangular building featured large picture windows, brick facing, and marble trim demarcating its steel structure. Reminiscent of Mies's work on the campus of the Illinois Institute of Technology in Chicago, the building's clean lines and lack of ornamentation was unusual for Greek housing, which usually favored more conservative Colonial or Tudor Revival styles. Woollen disagreed with that approach. "A good building housing seventy-two people cannot be successfully disguised as a one-family ranch or an antebellum confection," he told *Indiana Architect*, which featured the project on its cover.[21] An exposed staircase and trendy Herman Miller furniture completed the design's aesthetic.

The prismatic glass box was the archetypal modernist form: perfectly functional – but also rather severe. Its minimalism left little room for warmth or self-expression, never mind personal privacy amid all that glass and open space. While residents could try to soften their homes' hard edges with furnishings, there was only so much that could be done. Maybe that wasn't a bad thing. In an editorial titled "Future Is for People Who Live in Glass Houses," the *Indianapolis Star* begrudgingly welcomed the coming revolution: "Perhaps we need glass houses to make peaceable citizens. If we all lived in them, it might be that nobody would throw stones anymore."[22] However, as time went on, Woollen himself recognized the box's shortcomings. "Not all good houses are designed for coronary patients," he joked in 1960.[23]

He began to explore alternatives. One such experiment was a home he designed for Sylvan Perlov, a physician, and his family in the early 1960s. The house's layout expanded on the "big room concept" by bookending a main great room with two rectangular wings to form a U-shaped plan. The resulting central courtyard and a pitched, shingled roof was intended to reference the traditional architecture of Japan.[24] Inside, custom room dividers inspired by Japanese shoji screens provided flexible privacy. "We didn't want to live in a glass house on view to all the world," Perlov's wife told *House & Garden*.[25] A distinctive rug with a red and yellow diamond pattern, also designed by Woollen, brightened up the space.

The Leibman house, designed for Jordan and Joan Leibman, was even more unique. When the Leibmans first approached Woollen in 1959, the

***Above and below*:** Leibman House, 1964.

architect was initially reticent to accept the commission. He had just won the Clowes Memorial Hall project and had little time (or interest) in working on another starter home. Yet, sensing the couple's openness to new ideas, he decided to take the job and deliver a thoroughly unorthodox design. The home consisted of two cylindrical structures of slightly unequal size joined together by a shallow passageway (a third cylinder, for a garage, was designed but never built). The larger cylinder, containing the living room, kitchen, and primary bedroom, was for adults, while the smaller, featuring bedrooms and a playroom wrapped around a central laundry room, was designated for the Leibmans' young children. Both cylinders were capped by conical "top hats" clad in wood shingles.

A circular inversion of the modernist box, the plan was allegedly inspired by the fourteenth century stone huts, or *trulli*, that Woollen had encountered in Alberobello, Italy, during a postgraduate tour. Woollen also cited as inspiration the work of Wright and architect Bruce Goff, as well as a scheme for a much larger home of concentric circles, the Lucas residence, which he had worked on during his time in Johnson's studio.[26] Closer to home, there was also obvious resonance with the simple barns and rounded silos of the midwestern farm, leading writer Esther McCoy to declare in the pages of *Arts & Architecture* magazine that "the Leibman house is for the prairie."[27] Whatever the impetus, "it all added up to a feeling that I had to try," Woollen later said.[28] The Leibmans had never seen a round house before, but they happily accepted their architect's proposal. "He was prickly, but we always got along with him. He was easy to get along with if you just went along with him," remembered Joan Leibman, who lived in Woollen's creation for sixty years.[29] To further cut costs during construction, Jordan Leibman served as the general contractor at Woollen's request.

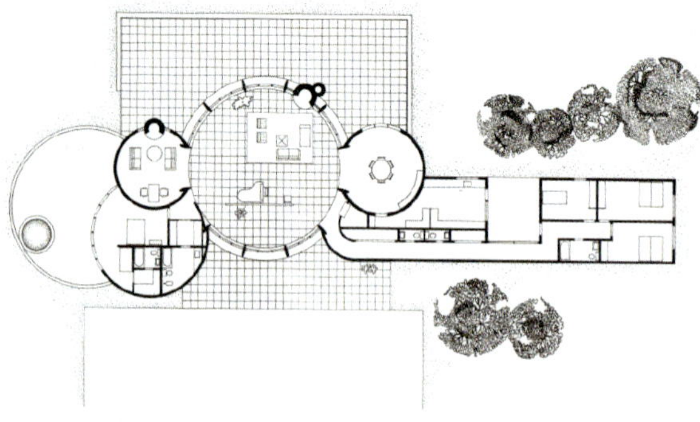

***Above*:**
Lucas House (unbuilt), designed by Philip Johnson, 1956.
Courtesy of Getty Research Library.

***Below*:**
Aerial view, Leibman House, 1964.

One of Woollen's last homes from this period was another example of the architect's interest in modern living beyond the glass box. It also showed what the architect could accomplish when a healthy budget was at hand. Tucked away in a wealthy northside neighborhood, the home was commissioned by Donald M. Mattison, the dynamic, Yale-trained director of Herron. Client and architect no doubt knew each other well; Woollen sat on Herron's board (so had his father and grandfather – it was something of a Woollen family tradition) and was also the architect for the school's new classroom building, Fesler Hall, completed in 1962. (During this same period, Woollen was also a central voice in heated discussions about the school's potential move to a larger, more suburban site outside the downtown area.)[30]

For his own home, Mattison requested an elegant design where he could entertain and display his art collection.[31] Woollen's solution, gracious and refined, was also highly idiosyncratic. In some ways it gestured towards New Formalism, a then-popular strain of classicized modernism, but also incorporated abstracted elements of the French Baroque style. While the home is an outlier in Woollen's portfolio (perhaps reflecting Mattison's personal tastes), its floor plan still centered around a familiar double-height room – albeit this time outfitted with marble floors, double doors, and porthole windows. The home's roofline was trapezoidal, a modernist

***Left and below*:**
Mattison House, 1964.

play on the traditionally French mansard roof, and clad in copper. Thoughtful details like angled brick edging and a limestone drip course provided horizontal balance to the roof's vertical thrust. Landscaping by the Dutch landscape designer Frits Loonsten further complemented its mannered forms. Terrifically preserved since its completion in 1964, the home was added to the National Register of Historic Places in 2022. A sensitive addition to the building's rear, also designed by Woollen, was built in 1990.

In all, Woollen designed approximately ten homes in Indianapolis during the first decade of his career. While arguably less unique or innovative than his later work, these projects remain rare and historically significant examples of midcentury modern domestic architecture in the city. But as Woollen put it later, "Architecture, in modern houses, was never of a great moment here."[32] Indianapolis just did not have the same appetite for glass-box living as places like New Canaan did. And for Woollen, larger – and more lucrative – commissions were on the horizon.

Clowes
Memor
Ha

Woollen in front of Clowes Memorial Hall, 1967.

Clowes Memorial Hall

1963 | Indianapolis, IN

In 1967 Robert Gover boarded a flight from Los Angeles to Indianapolis. On assignment for the *New York Times Magazine*, the writer and best-selling author was not exactly enthusiastic about his destination. What little he knew of Indianapolis, and the people who lived there, was less than positive. "I tend to refer to Hoosiers as Them, even as I admonish myself for such a baseless, nonexistent generality, for I developed an intense dislike for their rigid, conformist mores, their humorless provincialisms," he would later write, his words dripping with condescension.[1] "And now, inside the airport, I am stuck by the uniformity of clothing styles."

The subject of Gover's reporting trip: a recently completed performing arts center named Clowes Memorial Hall. Why this building was newsworthy depended on where you lived – and, therefore, who you were. For local residents the hall was an unprecedented piece of cultural infrastructure of a scale and ambition previously unknown in the city. Boasting twenty-two hundred seats, the tallest stage in the state, and a back of house large enough to accommodate four opera companies at once, the $3.5 million venue promised to put Indianapolis on the national cultural map. Equipped to host performances of all types, its size also meant that national touring productions could now finally make a stop in the city. "Showcasing noted talents only" promised its superlative-laden advertisements.[2]

But for the *Times*'s national readership, Clowes (pronounced "clues") was likely intriguing for an entirely different reason. Here was a major new arts institution of the highest caliber, not in a cosmopolitan metropolis like New York, Boston, or Los Angeles, but in Indianapolis. The theater's acoustics were acclaimed as industry leading, and an artistic committee of national stars – George Balanchine, Helen Hayes, Agnes DeMille, Arthur Rubenstein – advised on its programming.[3] Could this "hick hippodrome," as Gover cynically called it, really rival the country's great concert halls?[4]

The building's architecture was also part of the story. Wasn't Indianapolis supposed to be a city of strip malls, not architectural marvels? Clowes represented something different – a nine-story edifice of sheer Indiana limestone slabs held together by a concrete superstructure, at once elegant and ominous, ancient and ultramodern. Gover approved, writing: "I don't know what those imported operas and ballets have brought to the Hoosiers, but whoever created this building has brought them more than enough." Indianapolis had arrived. So had Clowes's architect, Evans Woollen.

The project that made the rest of Woollen's career possible, Clowes manifested the aspirations of a rapidly maturing city eager to assert itself on the national stage. It offered an exciting vision for Indianapolis's future and, at the same time, a compelling rebuttal to the negative stereotypes that had defined its past. As was made explicit on multiple occasions, the building's inspiration was no less than Lincoln Center, the sparkling new theater complex that had recently broken ground in New York City. At a cornerstone-laying ceremony for Clowes held in the fall of 1961, guests gathered to hear advice on their new construction project from Reginald Allen, Lincoln Center's vice president of operations, and Balanchine, the renowned choreographer whose New York City Ballet would soon be in residence there. To drive the matter home, copies of an article written by Allen titled "Lincoln Center Makes Its Case" were placed on the seat of every attendee.[5]

***Above*:**
Cornerstone-laying ceremony, 1961. Pictured are Woollen (*left*), Edith Clowes (*seated*), Allen Clowes (*holding program*), and George Bahre (*right*), the project's general contractor.

***Below*:**
Illustration of Clowes Memorial Hall, 1963.

Clowes's civic intent was important. Except for the old Murat Temple theater downtown, Indianapolis lacked a high-caliber theatrical venue, and calls for a "big, civic auditorium" worthy of the city's stature had been growing for some time.[6] Although Clowes would be built on the campus of Butler University, a small, private liberal arts college on Indianapolis's north side, its leaders expressly intended it as an amenity for all city residents. The project's main benefactor, philanthropist Edith Whitehill Hinkle Clowes, hoped the hall would become the new permanent home for the Indianapolis Symphony Orchestra (a tribute to her late husband, chemist and symphony supporter George Henry Alexander Clowes). Her gift of $2 million represented the largest donation ever to a cultural project in Indianapolis.[7] There was also conversation that the theater could anchor a new 580-acre cultural district that city leaders were planning for the land adjacent to Butler's campus.[8] When the *Indianapolis News* announced the project on May 29, 1959, the paper noted that "an architect of national prominence would be selected" to design the theater, further underscoring its expected significance.[9]

Woollen, then thirty-two, hardly fit that description. His portfolio at the time consisted of only a smattering of starter homes and bank branches. His office was barely an office at all but rather a "broom closet," as he described it later, "with just room for my drawing board and my own chair and a seat for a missing client."[10] He had never designed a theater before, and his first truly public building, Fesler Hall at the Herron School of Art, would not open until late 1962. But as was often the case in those early years, it was Woollen's family connections that got him in the door. His parents were friendly with Edith Clowes, and both the Woollen and the Clowes families were longtime patrons of Herron. Woollen himself was a personal acquaintance of Allen Clowes, Edith's youngest son, who would become the project's champion. When Allen approached Woollen about potentially submitting his credentials, the architect jumped at the chance.

There was, however, still the small problem of Woollen's résumé. The project demanded a famous name, not a hometown hero. Determined to win the commission, Woollen looked to his professional Rolodex for help – and hit on John Johansen, his friend and former employer in New Canaan, as the ideal collaborator.[11] The two would propose together for the project. While Johansen had not completed a theater either, he was about a decade older than Woollen and had more experience and notoriety. His work had been included in the influential *Built in U.S.A.: Post-war Architecture* exhibition at New York's Museum of Modern Art, and a major new commission, a US embassy building in Dublin, would soon start construction. But most important, Johansen was from Connecticut, not Indiana. His name brought a level of out-of-town prestige to their joint proposal that was not only helpful but essential; Woollen would later speculate that without Johansen's involvement, he would have likely lost the job.[12] "There is still a certain schizophrenia here that makes the Midwesterner overrate things from the outside world," Woollen would later tell Gover.[13]

In a document dated June 4, 1959, the two architects put forth their bid under the moniker "John M. Johansen and Evans Woollen III Associated Architects."[14] While Johansen's name was listed first, Woollen's Indianapolis address would be on their combined letterhead and where principal work would take place. To further sweeten their pitch, the two enlisted a group of world-class theater consultants to round out the team. These included the architectural lighting designer Richard Kelly; the theatrical lighting designer Jean Rosenthal; the seating designer Ben Schlanger; and the acousticians Bolt, Beranek & Newman. Uncoincidentally, all of these consultants also worked on Lincoln Center. (Rosenthal, Schlanger, and Bolt, Beranek & Newman would collaborate with Woollen again on the Musical Arts Center project.)

These were impressive credentials. Yet how Woollen and Johansen won the project seemed to do less with résumés and more with good timing and better manners. The story was recounted by Woollen often over the years and, whether factual or semi-apocryphal, it exemplified the layered dynamics of regionalism, identity, and taste at play. Woollen said,

> The interview just before us was Eero Saarinen, with wonderful experience. He had finished one of the great theaters in Lincoln Center. Mr. Saarinen was in a hurry. He was late for a jury for the Sydney Opera House and he was very interested in the Sydney Opera House. And he came, and throughout the interview he kept looking at his watch because he had a plane to catch to Sydney. Mrs. Clowes, who was of course a prime factor, probably the prime factor, was annoyed at his anxiety to leave. She wanted to get as much out of him as possible. The looking-at-the-clock, which, of course, was a great lesson to me to never look at the clock again, was distasteful to her. As we later heard it from Allen, it was the principal reason – can you believe it? – Eero Saarinen was not chosen. We came in after, without watches.[15]

On June 30, 1959, Woollen and Johansen were approved by Butler's board of trustees.[16] They were to be paid $170,000 for their efforts.

Clowes Memorial Hall, 1963.

The building that the two men designed together was a transformative addition to Indianapolis's architectural landscape and remains a high point of Woollen's career. Seemingly solid and porous at the same time, its facade was composed of individuated limestone totems held in place by exposed concrete frames to form a single crenelated image. Perfectly symmetrical when viewed head-on, the building dissolved into a "loose assemblage" of turrets and columns when glimpsed from other angles, an effect Woollen once likened to the collaged geometries of modern abstract art.[17] Elongated windows, tucked into the seams of the limestone slabs, provided interior light without interrupting the facade's planal rhythm. Relentlessly vertical, the building's only horizontal element was a raw concrete bulkhead placed above the front entrance, a modernist approximation of the traditional theater marquee.[18] (This element was substantially altered by a 2021 addition that added a front-facing window above the marquee and enclosed the space below it with glass.) At night Kelly's dramatic uplighting made the hall appear like a cubist fortress rising from the Indiana prairie.

Clowes is importantly understood as Woollen's first real outing in Brutalism, a then-new variance on modernism formulated by European architects like Le Corbusier and the British designers Alison and Peter Smithson.[19] Perhaps today more known for its negative public reception, Brutalism's original intent could be more neutrally defined as a blunt and visible structuralism, usually rendered through monumental scale and the liberal use of raw concrete (or *béton brut*, as Corbusier called it in French). It is unlikely Woollen or Johansen ever thought of themselves as explicitly "Brutalist" architects – instead, their approach was likely motivated more by mid-century notions of modernity, which valued honesty in construction and materials, as well as the unique plastic qualities of concrete. In the United States, Clowes stands as one of the style's early signal examples alongside far more famous works like Corbusier's Carpenter Center for the Visual Arts at Harvard University and Paul Rudolph's Yale Art & Architecture building, both of which were completed the same year as Clowes, as well as Louis Kahn's Richards Medical Research Laboratories at the University of Pennsylvania, completed slightly earlier in 1960.

After Clowes, Woollen would go on to work extensively in the Brutalist style; for better or for worse, his legacy remains closely associated with it. But at the time, Clowes's blocky, bulky design was a clear-cut departure from the type of architecture he had previously favored. Seemingly overnight Woollen had traded transparent glass for opaque concrete, simplistic form for composite structure. Although Woollen was always careful to position Clowes as the result of an equal collaboration between himself and Johansen, it is difficult not to see the older architect's outsized influence in the building's final appearance. Clowes's confident, sculptural exterior aligned well with Johansen's preference for strongly defined edifices, as well as his penchant for experimentation. Architecture was "an act," Johansen wrote in 1961, valuable only if "disruptive of the status quo and of professional tastes."[20] He was also particularly interested in concrete. A few years before winning the Clowes commission, Johansen debuted the "Spray House," an experimental, biomorphic dwelling formed from sprayed gunite. He would continue to bend concrete to his architectural will in subsequent projects like the embassy in Dublin and the now-demolished Morris A. Mechanic Theatre in Baltimore.

If anything, Woollen's sensitive touch was more apparent inside. Woollen had never designed a theater before, but he did have a good deal of experience *in* theaters as an actor and stagehand during his student days at Hotchkiss and Yale – so much so that he had even once flirted with becoming a professional set designer. He approached the interior with the understanding that audience members were performers in their own right, and their experience deserved its own choreography. From the hall's front door, ticket holders were welcomed into an unusually large wraparound lobby. Rafts of balconies on the upper floors were perfectly constructed for a see-and-be-seen evening, while towering concrete pylons framed the entire tableau. The concrete's industrial sensibility was somewhat softened by two important design elements: lush wall-to-wall carpet designed by Woollen and Edith

Clowes in a chartreuse hexagonal pattern; and a seventeenth-century Flemish tapestry, borrowed from the Clowes family's personal collection and mounted proudly on the lobby's largest wall.[21] Despite these accommodations, Woollen knew the use of exposed concrete in the interior of a luxury theater would likely be a bitter pill for his fellow Hoosiers to swallow. "The biggest single hurdle for Indianapolis to get over will be the raw concrete interior," he predicted to the *Indianapolis News* before the building had opened.[22] Nonetheless, he said, "The more people travel, the more they will see this material used."

In the theater's house, a luxurious seventy-foot curtain made of crimson velvet greeted audience members as they found their seats. Lighting and surface colors throughout were carefully calibrated to evoke "a great lantern," as Woollen later called it – "beautiful to photograph and beautiful to be in."[23] The lobby carpet transitioned to a palette of yellows, reds, and browns. Above, acoustical panels hung from the ceiling like golden clouds. There was no central aisle; instead, seats were arranged in the

***Above*:**
Lobby interior, ca. 1963.

***Left*:**
Theater interior and stage, ca. 1963.

CLOWES MEMORIAL HALL
4602

RESERVED

***Above*:**
Irwin Library, designed by Minoru Yamasaki, 1963. J. Irwin Miller and his relatives, Clementine Tangeman and Elsie Irwin Sweeney, stand in front.

***Below*:**
Existing campus buildings, Butler University.

"continental style" like the great European concert halls, allowing for more center seats and less interrupted views. It was only inside the house that one understood the overall program as a "building within a building": the theater auditorium as a central nucleus, the lobby wrapped snugly around its form, and the exterior stone facade as a final, protective layer. Woollen would continue to emphasize this exterior-interior dialectic in subsequent projects, most especially the Musical Arts Center at Indiana University.

That Woollen and Johansen were successful in bringing such a building to life was a testament to their ambition and ingenuity as designers. It also showed their deftness in handling their clients. While Butler had a somewhat progressive reputation pedagogically, the school's appetite for architectural innovation was, by Woollen's estimation, "very conservative."[24] While choosing Woollen and Johansen for the commission, Butler's trustees also passed a resolution explicitly stipulating that the new theater could not be "out of coordination" with the campus's existing Collegiate Gothic architecture – a directive that put immediate limits on what Woollen and Johansen might conceive.[25] The architects instead used this restriction to their advantage, skillfully molding their design into a sort of modern reinterpretation of the Gothic style with a similar stony exterior and strong vertical thrust. As the design work neared completion in late 1959, one trustee predicted that Clowes would be a "beautiful cathedral" and maybe even "one of the most wonderful buildings in America."[26] Woollen would embrace this type of context-driven approach even more fully in his later work.

Ironically, the trustees' demand for "coordination" also seemed to include accounting for campus buildings that had not yet been built – specifically, a new library planned for across the quad. The library was to be designed by Minoru Yamasaki, the prominent Detroit-based architect, and funded by the Irwin-Miller-Sweeney Foundation of Columbus, Indiana. J. Irwin Miller, the foundation's head, sat on Butler's board and was in all likelihood responsible for Yamasaki's selection.[27] Although Miller was not directly involved in the Clowes project, he was active in conversations about the overall architectural character of Butler's campus, going so far as to author an eight-point "Architectural Policy of the University," which was adopted by his fellow trustees in 1960.[28] Perhaps it was Miller who pushed for the "coordination" requirement in the hopes that his library would not be overshadowed by the Brutalist theater being planned for at the same time. At the trustees' request, Woollen traveled to Yamasaki's office to discuss the matter personally. "[Yamasaki] gave me a lecture about how libraries were the most important buildings on campus, and the theater should not rival it in any way," Woollen remembered later, recalling how Yamasaki sat "on a dais" during the meeting and had tea served to himself but not to his guest.[29] It is unclear whether the trustees demanded Yamasaki pay Woollen and Johansen a similar visit. Yamasaki's library, designed in the New Formalist style with a facade of white barrel vaults, opened in September 1963 just a few weeks before Clowes did.

Although Woollen and Johansen would remain friends, Clowes was to be their only collaboration. "Philosophically, our practices after Clowes verged somewhat," Woollen said later. "I was very interested in the ethos of the place where the building was. Joe was not really taken with that."[30] There is, however, evidence that the two men did attempt to work together on at least one other project, confirmed by a sketch held in the Indiana State Library titled "A very preliminary study for a Lincoln Memorial in Indiana." The sketch, dated 1959, shows a solitary statue of a young Abraham Lincoln placed on a raised court in front of a diaphanous pavilion. An accompanying memo sets out the goals of the program with the same thoughtfulness that the two architects brought to Clowes: "The assumption has been that to be appropriate such a memorial should be simple, strong, slightly romantic, informal hence asymmetrical, and heroic. It has also been assumed that a monument in 1960 to a man in 1830, cannot be built as a pioneer cabin or a greek or gothic revival temple, but must use the present day vernacular to be as honest as Lincoln himself."[31] The document was typed on Woollen's office stationery but with the names "Evans Woollen" and "John M. Johansen" written by hand at the bottom. Likely connected to Lincoln sesquicentennial celebrations from around this same time, the project was never built.[32]

Clowes Memorial Hall opened in October 1963 to great fanfare with a slate of diverse programming, including Bob Hope, Captain Kangaroo, and a performance by members of the Bolshoi Ballet. Festivities kicked off with a black-tie celebration for the city's elite, televised live from the lobby's hexagonal carpet as if the event were the Academy Awards. "It was a great occasion for Indianapolis," Woollen remembered, "with huge searchlights and valet parking and cars lined up and ladies getting out of backseats in their finery and going into the hall. . . . My wife and I owned a car that was

Sketch for Abraham Lincoln Memorial, 1959.
Courtesy of the Indiana State Library.

Architectural Forum, December 1963.
Illustration by Pieter Brattinga.

somewhat out-of-date. I remember the people in my office were very concerned that the car would look shabby in front of the television cameras."[33] Edith Clowes, the guest of honor, wore a white ball gown with matching wool coat.[34]

With the project complete, Johansen returned home to Connecticut, leaving Woollen in Indianapolis to face the reviews. Public response was "mixed, at first," Woollen told Gover. "A few city fathers wanted to tear up the seating and install a central aisle, and another group of conservatives wanted to paint the concrete exterior gold. It seemed pretty rough to them at first. But now they accept it."[35] If the reception at home was initially lukewarm, national press coverage was plentiful, and positive. *Architectural Forum* put the project on its December 1963 cover, while *Fortune* named it one of "ten buildings that point the future" alongside now-seminal works by Mies van der Rohe, Rudolph, and, ironically, Saarinen.[36]

Nonetheless, stereotypes of Indiana as a cultural backwater were hard to shake. When *Time* magazine included Clowes in a long article on the nation's new "pavilions of culture," it was sure to note that the hall's "fine backstage facilities, adjustable-size stage and superb acoustics have made Indianapolis one of the prime stopovers for shows on the road, whereas there used to be a saying that 'the two worst weeks in the year were Christmas and Indianapolis.'"[37] Only Johansen's name was listed as architect, prompting Woollen to write a letter to the editor asking for a correction: "Sir: Does TIME know that two architects designed Clowes Hall?" he inquired.[38]

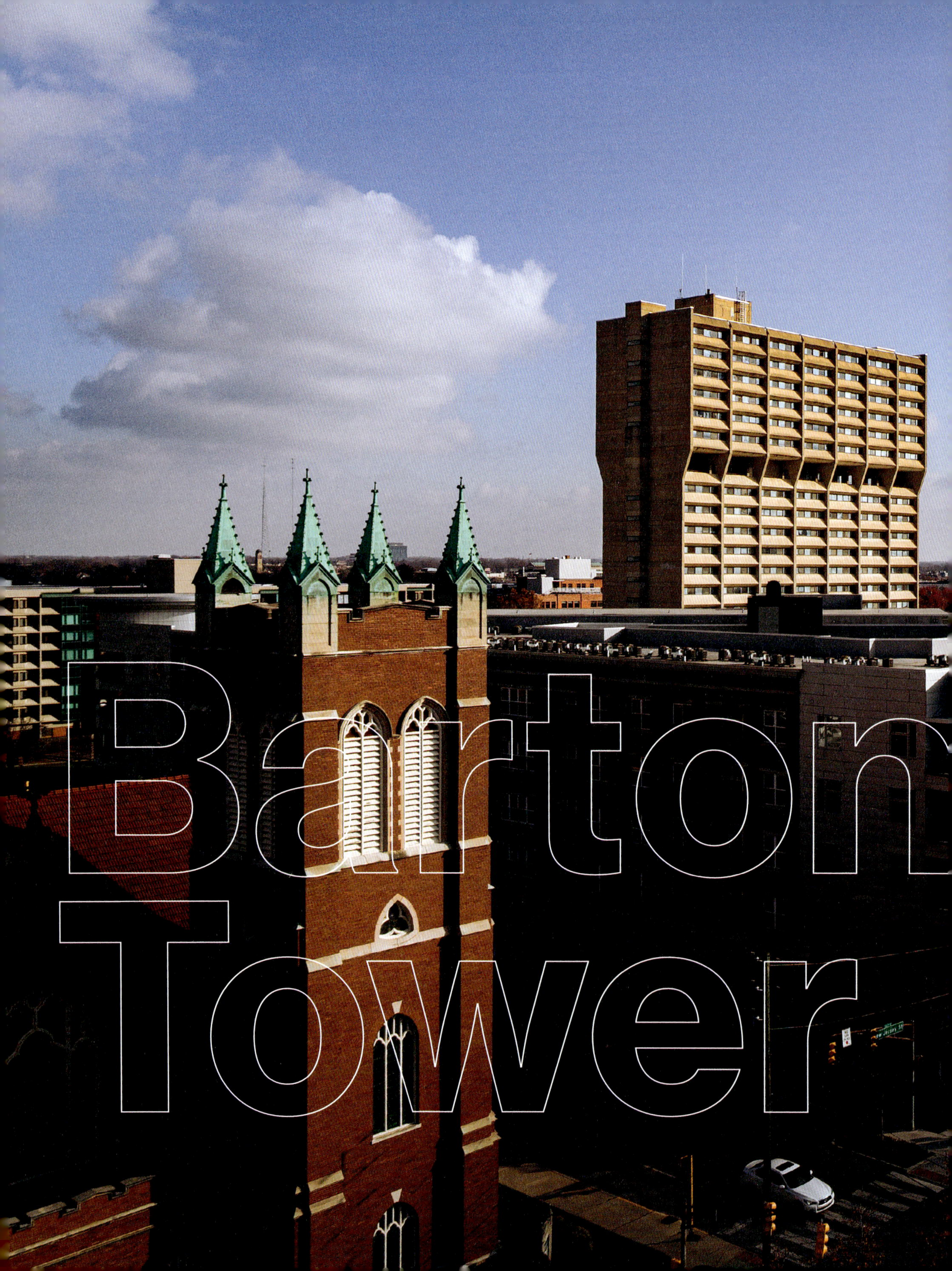

Barton Tower

North St
Murat & Shriners

***Above*:**
Barton Tower and skybridge as seen from Massachusetts Avenue, ca. 1990.

***Below*:**
Demolition of Barton Tower skybridge, 1995.

John J. Barton Apartments

1968 | Indianapolis, IN

It was a cloudy, early summer morning in 1995 when the wrecking crew took its first swing at the John J. Barton Tower apartment complex. Once a symbol of Indianapolis's urban progress, the public housing project had certainly seen better days. Vacancy was pushing 30 percent, and residents complained of crime and overdue maintenance. The building's hard-edged Brutalism, previously the style of choice for government housing, now felt like it belonged to another era. "The apartments, as they are designed, are no longer applicable to the lifestyle of Indianapolis," declared Mayor Stephen Goldsmith.[1]

An $8 million renovation would modernize Barton for the new needs of Indianapolis. And according to the mayor, that meant removing one of the building's signature design elements, a dramatic, four-story concrete span that connected the complex's main tower to a smaller, eight-story annex building across the street. The Indianapolis Pacers were facing off against the Orlando Magic that evening, and a public demolition only added to the city's excitement. As Goldsmith himself swung the wrecking ball into the graffiti-covered bridge, cries of "Boom baby!" (the Pacers' famous catchphrase) rose up from the crowd.[2]

There was no doubt that Barton needed an upgrade. But in the eyes of city leadership (and more than a few Indianapolis residents), there was another problem: the building was ugly. Seemingly chiseled out of bland, beige concrete, its severe design and inhuman scale played into the worst stereotypes of low-income housing. The infamous skybridge was the target of particular ire, and housing officials reasoned it would be cheaper to tear it down than try to rehabilitate it. Evans Woollen be damned; Barton's architectural pedigree was irrelevant if no one wanted to live there. "The Barton Apartments might be significant for its period to some people, but other people find it atrocious, ugly. I don't know that I have to agree with those who like it just because it appeared in a magazine article," one housing official told the *Indianapolis Star*.[3]

Barton was Woollen's first major job in Indianapolis's downtown core, and it offered the architect a new and exciting challenge: designing for the masses. "People are dynamite," he said in 1967.[4] "[Barton] is a lot more exciting than doing a factory or a place where people don't want to live." Conceived during the administration of Democratic mayor John J. Barton as part of a broader push toward urban rehabilitation following World War II, the building would be the city's first public housing project in three decades, designated to serve downtown's elderly and most vulnerable with a degree of safety, dignity, and considered design. With a budget of only $3.9 million, Woollen was tasked with fitting 247 government-subsidized units on a small, triangular lot along Massachusetts Avenue, at the time a generally impoverished area with a mix of storefront businesses, brick apartment flats, and wood-framed homes.[5] His solution was highly utilitarian: Six floors of larger, two-person apartments stacked on top of thirteen floors of smaller, one-person apartments, resulting in a Y-shaped tower that was wider at the top than at the bottom. Double-loaded corridors optimized budget and space, but the building's east–west orientation – angled toward the center of downtown like "a baffle" – ensured all units received morning or afternoon light.[6]

Extensive use of raw concrete, Woollen's material of choice during the 1960s, also kept cost down. The tower's confident, even defiant formalism was quickly becoming a hallmark for the architect.

Barton Tower (*left*), skybridge (*center*), and annex building (*right*), 1971.

While Clowes Memorial Hall is usually regarded as Woollen's first Brutalist design, it was Barton that more obviously embraced the rugged structuralism of Le Corbusier's *béton brut,* its craggy seams and irregular pockmarks left proudly visible in the Brutalist mode. Raking slab spandrels, described by the press as a "pregnant venetian blind," were precast and then assembled in place to form the tower's distinctive geometric facade.[7]

Although new for Indianapolis, Barton belonged to a wave of mass housing projects constructed across the United States during the postwar era. They ranged from single buildings like Barton to whole neighborhoods of housing towers, such as the infamous Pruitt-Igoe complex completed in St. Louis in 1955. Often presaged by the government-mandated displacement of existing residents, these projects marshaled modernist theories of architecture and urban planning in hopes of alleviating deteriorating conditions in downtown areas. For many modern architects, the multifamily housing typology was a productive site for rethinking, sometimes radically, the organization of society following the destruction of World War II. Woollen was clearly abreast of these developments: In a 1967 lecture at Ball State University in Muncie, Indiana, he noted some of the futuristic housing ideas, like Archigram's speculative Plug-In City or Moshe Safdie's concrete Habitat 67 in Montreal, that were on his mind at the time of Barton's creation. He also discussed at length Le Corbusier, a key figure in the development of twentieth-century urbanism, whom he deemed "*the* architect of the twentieth century, at least as we know it. It's taken me a long time to come to that conclusion."[8]

Indeed, Barton reflects the deep influence Corbusier had on Woollen's work during this period. Its design has often been compared to Corbusier's famous *Unité d'habitation* project, completed in Marseille in 1952. Both were monolithic concrete housing blocks, reflective of the "tower in the park" typology that Corbusier and others believed to be the future of collective living. The brightly painted panels that decorated Barton's skybridge were also a clear reference to similar decoration on Corbusier's building. Barton was just one of several homages Woollen made to Corbusier during this same period. In 1969 the firm's unsuccessful competition entry for a new architecture building at Ball State clearly recalled the Swiss architect's concrete

***Above*:**
Model of Ball State University Architecture Building (unbuilt), 1967.

***Below*:**
Model of a mixed-use apartment building (unbuilt), 1969.

work, as did other, today little-known designs like the Rotz Engineering building in Speedway, Indiana; an unbuilt mixed-use tower planned for downtown Bloomington, Indiana; and the first design proposal for the New Harmony Inn in New Harmony, Indiana.

Barton's utopian airs had surprising resonance in Indianapolis, a planned city with its own pronounced history of urban self-invention. Its founding urban plan – in place almost as soon as the city was established in 1821 by government decree – was a remarkable vision of Cartesian geometry, a square-mile gridiron thoughtfully oriented to the cardinal directions. The "Mile Square plan," as it is still known today, was the work of two men: Elias Pym Fordham, a British civil engineer, and Alexander Ralston, a Scotsman who had previously assisted in the planning of Washington, DC. While the nation's capital was much larger than Indianapolis, Fordham and Ralston imbued their design for this new Midwestern city with a similar idealistic grandeur.[9] The scheme was notable for the four diagonal boulevards that cut through the plan's grid, terminating at a central circular lot earmarked for a future governor's residence. Other prominent spaces were also allocated for civic structures the city hoped would eventually materialize.

The plan's ambition befitted the city's invented name, "Indianapolis" – basically a statement of intent for the kind of classical ideal that state leaders (including Woollen's ancestor Samuel Merrill, to whom the name is sometimes attributed) intended to erect out of what was then dense forestland. Such aggrandizing mythology would continue during Woollen's time, becoming a sort of self-fulfilling prophecy that fueled the city's modern growth. "Indianapolis is a city built upon plans made by hardy pioneers bent upon creating a social order as well as a fine state capitol," wrote the Indianapolis Chamber of Congress in a 1970 promotional brochure, drawing a bright line between the city's nineteenth-century founding and its twentieth-century renewal. "About Indianapolis there is no element of circumstance either in the selection of its site or the design for the original town. And today, as from the beginning, it is a city planned in its development," it declared.[10]

Barton belonged to this next chapter in Indianapolis's ongoing story of self-fulfillment. The war effort had left physical infrastructure to languish, and by 1945 the downtown area was by all accounts a derelict shadow of its former self. "Even those of us who are enthusiastically civic minded will admit that Indianapolis is a dirty, smoky place in which to live," declared the Indianapolis Post-War Planning Committee, a government-appointed coalition of local business leaders tasked with evaluating the city's condition.[11] Their assessment, issued in 1946, painted a dire picture: failing sewage systems, gridlocked streets, and overburdened public amenities. In particular, the city's existing housing stock – of the kind Barton would effectively replace – was "breeding grounds for disease, juvenile delinquency and low standards of living." It's possible that a teenage Woollen was at least tangentially aware of the committee's work, as his father served on the group's finance subcommittee.[12]

The 1862 Marion County Courthouse, designed by Isaac Hodgson, seen mid-demolition. Behind it stands the new City-County Building designed by Wright, Porteous and Associates, 1962.

Although a similar story was unfolding in cities across the country, Indianapolis's problems appeared to be particularly acute. In 1948 the *Saturday Evening Post* dispatched two writers to the Hoosier capital who reported back that both "the loveliest homes" and "the most hideous slums in the United States" could be found there.[13] "The people of Indianapolis are considerably more attractive than much of the town they live in," they concluded. Unsurprisingly, such conditions led to a marked population decrease in the inner city and a boom in suburban areas. In 1900, 85 percent of county residents lived in Center Township, an area roughly equal to Indianapolis. By 1950, 64 percent did.[14] Urgent action was needed. The committee recommended a $25 million road map for Indianapolis's turnaround: "slum clearance" and urban renewal; the creation of new highway infrastructure; and the construction of new housing, offices, retail, and schools. The city would enact all these changes and more over the coming decades.

What would Indianapolis's next chapter look like? While the committee did not give much attention to matters of design, the city's architectural community had been dreaming about new possibilities for some time. In the 1950s and 1960s, a series of speculative plans – some endorsed by the city's newly created planning department, others sponsored by local businesses – sketched out visionary (and often naive) proposals for Indianapolis's future. In every plan the city was imagined as a far more dense, cosmopolitan, and lively place than its current reality, filled with thriving businesses, bustling shops, and happy pedestrians. Modernism was claimed as the city's de facto urban identity, replacing the ornate Victorian and neoclassical architecture for which the downtown Indianapolis was originally known. Streets were lined with uninterrupted glass frontage, and moving sidewalks whisked urbanites to and from their destinations. One plan, called *Indianapolis Centrum*, proposed redirecting the White River into the heart of the city to create an urban shorefront similar to Chicago's and constructing a Corbusian "dream town" of housing towers in a new public park.[15] While Woollen was clear-eyed about *Indianapolis Centrum*'s lack of feasibility, he liked its ambition: "It's easy to criticize this plan. I'm very happy that it was done, and I think it should be stimulating to anybody who looks at it, whether they agree with everything or not. This is what cities the size of Indianapolis or Muncie or any place ought to have at frequent intervals," he said in his 1967 lecture at Ball State.[16]

In the real world, change came more incrementally but no less forcefully. Although Indianapolis never accepted federal funding for urban renewal at the same scale as cities like Boston or Pittsburgh, both of which were well-known for their aggressive urban renewal projects, its efforts to remake its public realm were still significant.[17] And like in Boston or Pittsburgh, architectural design was an important marker of the coming era. If Indianapolis purported to be a "modern" city (as the reasoning went), it ought to look like one. Building by building, its nineteenth-century character was replaced by the slick aesthetic of twentieth-century design. Modernist office towers, like the Fidelity Building (1959), the City-County Building (1962), and the Indiana National Bank Building (1970) – newly minted as the state's tallest structure – beckoned workers and businesses back into the downtown core. Stylish retail, epitomized by the curvilinear J. C. Penney store (1952) designed by Skidmore, Owings, & Merrill, offered an elevated shopping experience. Hotels, like the new Hilton (1970) with its glass-fronted elevator, catered to out-of-town travelers attending events at the city's new convention center (1972). "No longer could Fortune Magazine use a front cover photo of a stoplight in a cornfield to represent Indianapolis. We've grown up," proudly reported the *Indianapolis News*.[18]

Indianapolis entered a state of near-constant construction. Demolitions became public spectacles, with bleachers erected in front of job sites so that locals could cheer on the changes for themselves (an ironic premonition of Barton's own public destruction decades later).[19] Sometimes whole neighborhoods were erased. Near Barton's future site, the city razed some forty-two acres in a predominantly Black neighborhood to make room for the James Whitcomb Riley Center (now known as Riley Towers), a privately funded "apartment city" designed by the Chicago firm Perkins & Will. Although only its first phase was completed, Perkins & Will's original plan called for four thirty-story towers and six sixteen-story towers, plus a conglomeration of retail, restaurants, and other luxury amenities all within its walled and terraced confines. The project promised to be "a new horizon in Indianapolis," as one advertisement claimed in 1963, a cloistered urban playground specifically targeted toward the white, middle-class resident otherwise alienated by the city's so-called blight.[20]

An important precursor to Barton, the Riley Center was hailed as a game changer – "the greatest visual and social stride in the heart of the city since the World War Memorial plaza was laid out in the 1920s," Woollen himself declared.[21] *Indiana Architect* featured the project on its May 1963 cover, showing one of the center's towers under construction and, dramatically, a dilapidated older structure crumbling before it. A poignant image of the new rising from the ashes of the old, the illustration's caption read simply, "Progress." Progress, however, would not be evenly distributed; the magazine failed to mention that the neighborhood's

Cross Roads Plan

Edward D. Pierre, 1953

Commissioned by local department store L. Strauss & Co., the Cross Roads Plan was the brainchild of architect Edward D. Pierre, a longtime advocate for the restoration of downtown Indianapolis. Seeking to alleviate the city's notoriously bad traffic, the plan proposed (among other ideas) four enormous parking structures that would function as car-centered gateways into the downtown core. After parking, motorists could then use subways, underground buses, and even moving sidewalks to traverse the city.

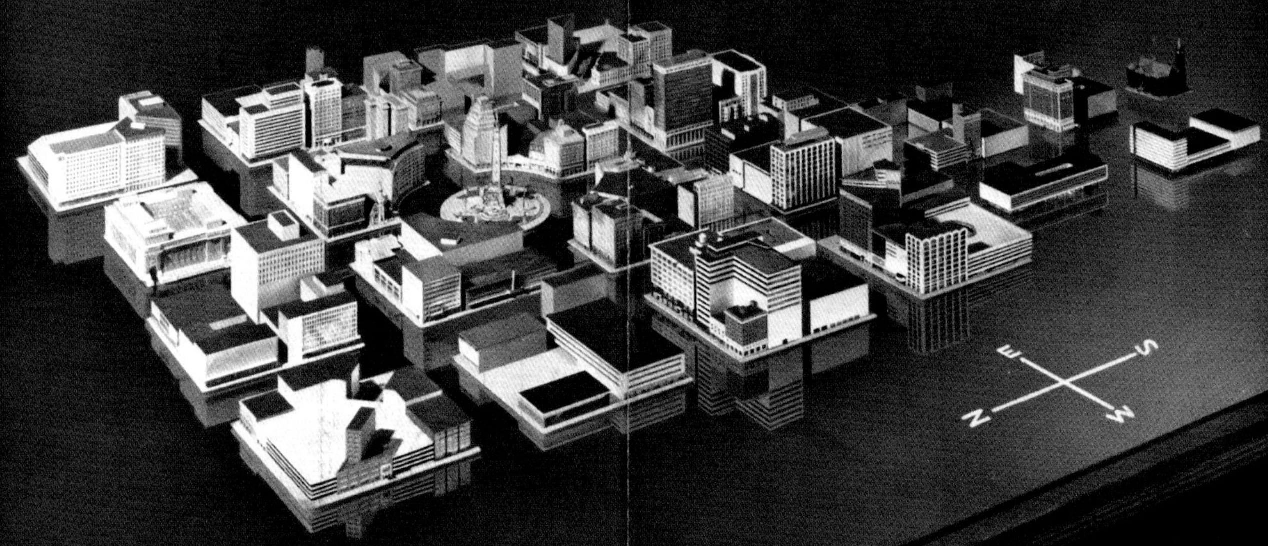

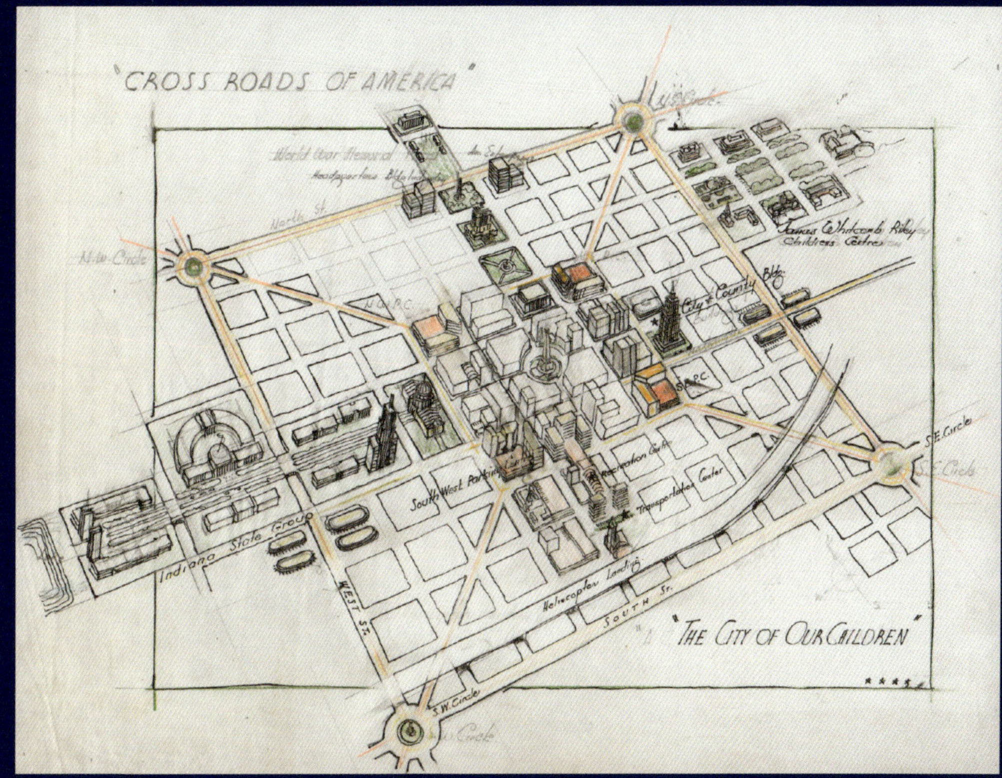
"CROSS ROADS OF AMERICA"
"THE CITY OF OUR CHILDREN"
Indiana State Group
WEST ST.
SOUTH ST.
Helicopter Landing
South-West Parking Centre
Transportation Center
S.E. Circle
S.W. Circle
James Whitcomb Riley Childrens Centre
City + County Bldg.

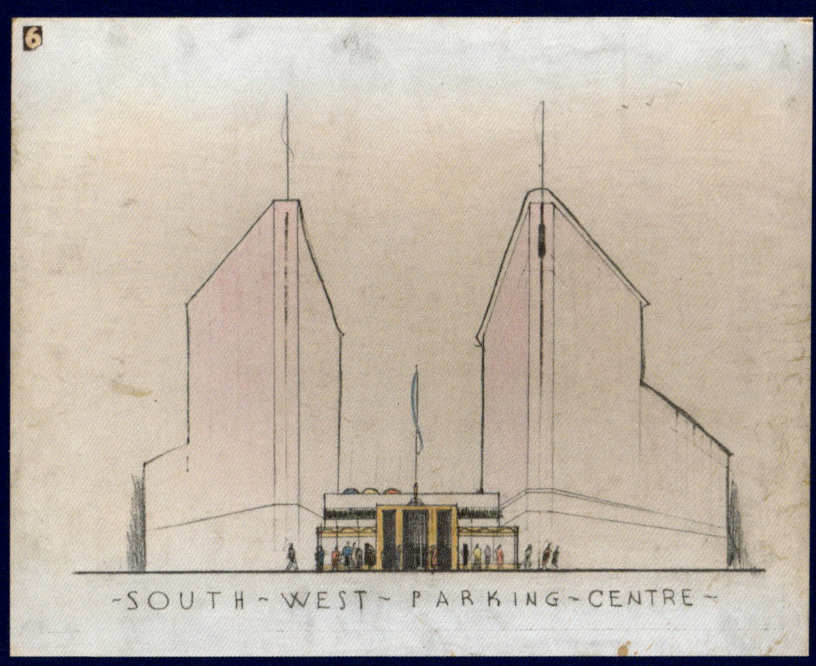
6
-SOUTH-WEST-PARKING-CENTRE-

Central Business District Report

Department of Metropolitan Development, 1955

The Central Business District report represented the hopes and dreams of Indianapolis's newly created planning department, incorporated in 1955. Building on Pierre's Cross Roads Plan, the report put forth a vision of modern Indianapolis with defined urban districts, a closed-loop freeway, consolidated government facilities, and large-scale urban renewal. Its authors contended that an investment in downtown Indianapolis would ensure the city could compete with places like Philadelphia, Pittsburgh, and Chicago. The report also emphasized design excellence and noted that "architectural competition should be held on a national, as well as a local and regional basis, to insure truly good design."

Images courtesy of City of Indianapolis, Department of Metropolitan Development.

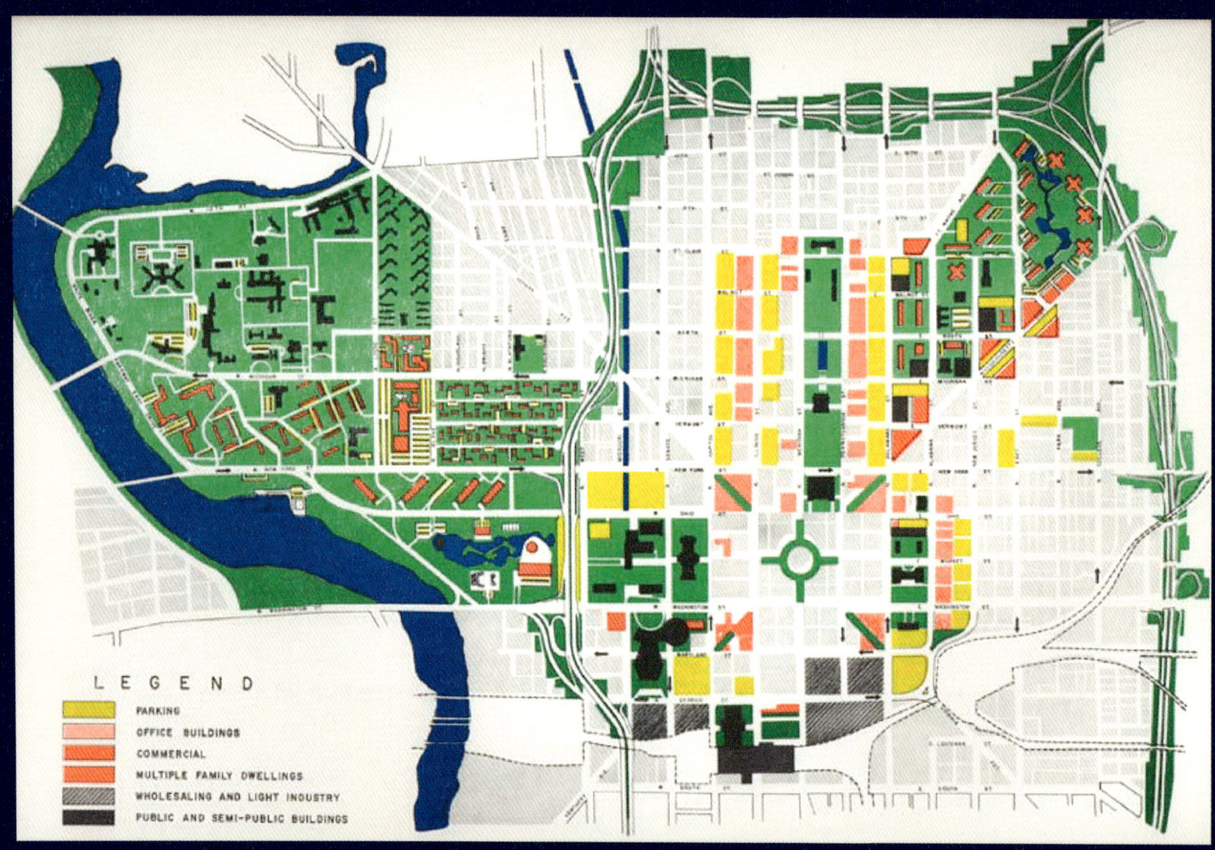

CBD
indianapolis

MICHIGAN STREET
TOWER APARTMENTS
UNIVERSITY HOUSING
GREEN OPEN SPACE
SURFACE PARKING
ELEMENTARY SCHOOL
TERRACE HOUSING
OPEN AIR MARKET
SURFACE PARKING
COMMERCIAL PLAZA
TRANSPORATION CENTER
TOWER APARTMENTS
ROOF TOP RECREATION
PROFESSIONAL SERVICES
PEDESTRIAN MOVEMENT
NEW YORK STREET
SHOPPING AND ENTERTAINMENT
COMMUNITY SOCIAL CENTER
JUNIOR HIGH SCHOOL
RECREATION FIELDS
AMPHITHEATER
MARINA
WHITE RIVER

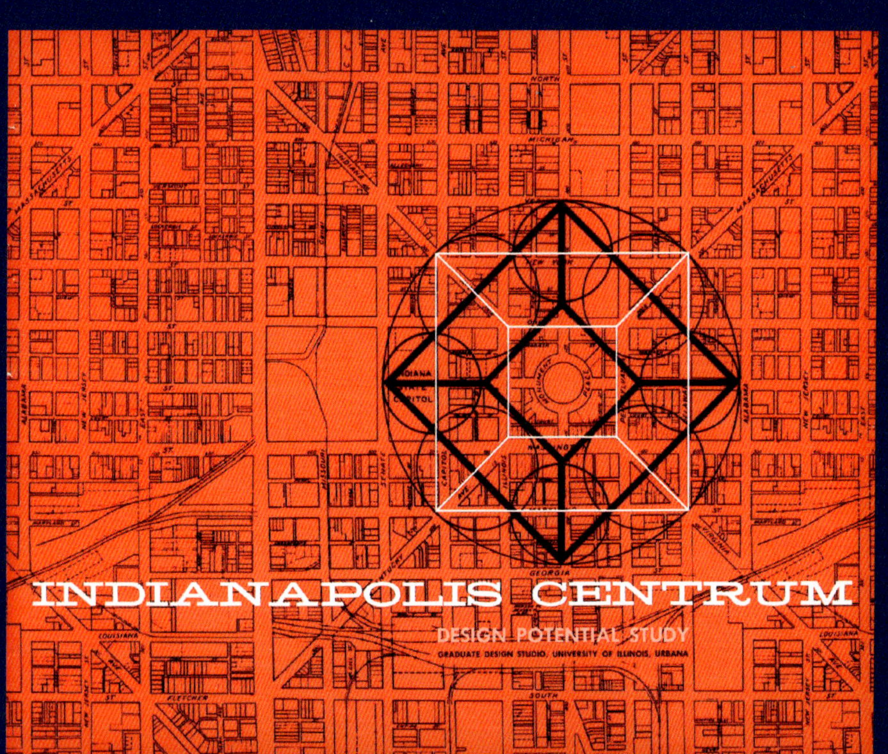
INDIANAPOLIS CENTRUM
DESIGN POTENTIAL STUDY
GRADUATE DESIGN STUDIO, UNIVERSITY OF ILLINOIS, URBANA

Barton Tower residents, ca. 1968. The towers of Riley Center can be seen at right in the distance.

original residents would now be priced out of the luxury apartments on offer.[22]

The Riley Center represented one vision for downtown Indianapolis's future. Barton was another, and vital in its own way. The Post-War Planning Committee had identified housing as one of the city's critical deficits, and as local leaders intensified their urban renewal activities, more and more lower-income residents evicted by the so-called paths of progress would need to be rehoused.[23] Barton would help, and also provide a first testing ground for Woollen's urbanist philosophies. Woollen contended that livable and enduring cities did not happen by accident; rather, it was the architect's duty to help shape a better urban realm. By his estimation the hollowing of cities was a product of planners and politicians failing to understand what humans really wanted from their cities: connectivity, community, and belonging.

In 1966 Woollen laid out his thoughts on the topic in an editorial published by *Indiana Architect* titled "If Cities Prevail." Despite the ambivalence of its title, the article offered a strong defense for the city's future. Among many other recommendations, Woollen challenged architects to think about urbanity in a more holistic, human-centered way. "[The consumer] would stop running from the city when the benefits of a return are evident. It would take more than ordinances to reverse this tide; it would take an effective social unit larger than the half-acre ranch. The feeling of one's neighborhood could be like coming and going from rooms of a large house," Woollen wrote (this last sentence seeming to anticipate Louis Kahn's own statements about the "room as the beginning of architecture" and the street as a "room by agreement").[24] Here, Woollen diverged from the Cobusian notion of a purely rational urbanism, instead seeing the city as Kahn and Jane Jacobs (another influence) did: as a living thing, made for people, growing and changing in a constant, joyful flux.

When Barton opened in 1968, it had no trouble attracting tenants. The complex was at full occupancy within a year, with three thousand more on a waiting list.[25] "The Barton Towers are a bright spot and serve a crying need," reported one local housing nonprofit, noting median rent as $33 compared to $58 in the surrounding area.[26] "Isn't this just wonderful? I can't believe it. I'm living like a queen," a new resident told the *Indianapolis Star*.[27] *Architectural Forum* ran a six-page spread documenting the finished design under the somewhat absurdist headline "Palazzo Vecchio, Indiana Style." The text likened the tower's "assertive silhouette and rugged texture" to an Italian campanile.[28] Clearly proud of the project's coverage by a prestigious national magazine, Woollen sent the *Forum* article to then mayor Richard Lugar, who received it enthusiastically.[29] The project also received international exposure through its inclusion in an architecture exhibition staged in the American Pavilion at the 1970 Japan World Exposition. Depicted by a striking photograph from the Magnum photographer Elliott Erwitt, Barton hung alongside approximately one hundred other images of both modern and historic buildings, a sort of visual census of the nation's most important architectural achievements.[30]

As a result of Barton's popularity, the city soon engaged Woollen to build an additional annex across the street. The expansion would increase the development's capacity by 258 units. This was when Woollen proposed the skybridge, providing residents passage between the original tower and the annex and forming a U-shaped plan spread across two city lots. The bridge connected to the tower like an ungainly appendage, recalling Archigram's idea of "plug-in" architecture that was modular and endlessly extendable. A small park formed in the complex's elbow offered tenants valuable green space while giving the whole project a more enclosed, campus-like feel (albeit still open to the surrounding urban context). More press followed, and the project was subsequently featured in Ivan Chermayeff's

Barton Tower apartment interior, ca. 1968.

Observations on American Architecture (where the building was attributed to "Evans Woolen") and G. E. Kidder Smith's *The Architecture of the United States: An Illustrated Guide to Notable Buildings*. "Any architect who can survive the bureaucracy of the public housing gauntlet in the U.S.A. deserves to be congratulated, especially if he arrives at a solution as capable as this," wrote Smith.[31]

However it is unclear what Barton's residents truly thought of their new home. The very notion of high-rise housing – domestic living suspended two hundred feet in the air – was still seen as a new and unsettling idea, rife with danger or at the very least vertigo. The *Indianapolis Star* reported that even the Riley Center had struggled to convince "far more youthful and venturesome" tenants to move into its tower units.[32] How would Barton's elderly residents fare at such heights? "Some of them will probably be terrified by it all," predicted Harrison J. Ullman, the *Star*'s science writer.[33] Suggesting that high-rise living carried with it a mental health risk, he concluded that "the old folks' high-rise [Barton] may be daring and innovative architecture and still be a bad place for poor elderly citizens to live."

Assuming Barton's aged tenants could stomach the elevation, they would also need to reckon with

Woollen's Brutalist aesthetic. Pictures from the time show interior rooms as sparse and unadorned, with small windows and exposed concrete walls. While occupants could add warmth with their own rugs and furniture, it was likely hard to escape the fact that they were living in glorified concrete cells. This was not necessarily Woollen's fault alone, and he even noted that units were necessarily minimalist due to government requirements.[34] But like Woollen's private homes from the previous decade, it was easy to argue that style had trumped comfort. A long, arcaded balcony on the tower's fifteenth floor offered residents expansive views of downtown, but there was little to look at in the immediate vicinity except for a patchwork of surface parking lots and active construction sites.[35] Like a concrete sentinel, Barton loomed over it all.

Barton represented Woollen's first attempt at designing for urban life on a truly meaningful scale. Yet as its skybridge crumbled that early summer morning in 1995, it was difficult to say that the architect's experiment was wholly successful. However admirable its intent, Barton – and the rationales behind it – would go the way of so many public housing projects of its era, a fall from fashion spurred on by changing tastes and government divestment. After decades of struggle, today Barton's neighborhood is a thriving mix of restaurants, retail, and low-rise apartment buildings catering to young professionals. And while Barton still stands, its original design intent has been altered beyond recognition. In 2013 new construction encircling the tower's base effectively severed its relationship to the street, cutting off entrances and filling in the open green space integral to Woollen's overall vision.[36] Barton's sublimation was complete, no wrecking ball required.

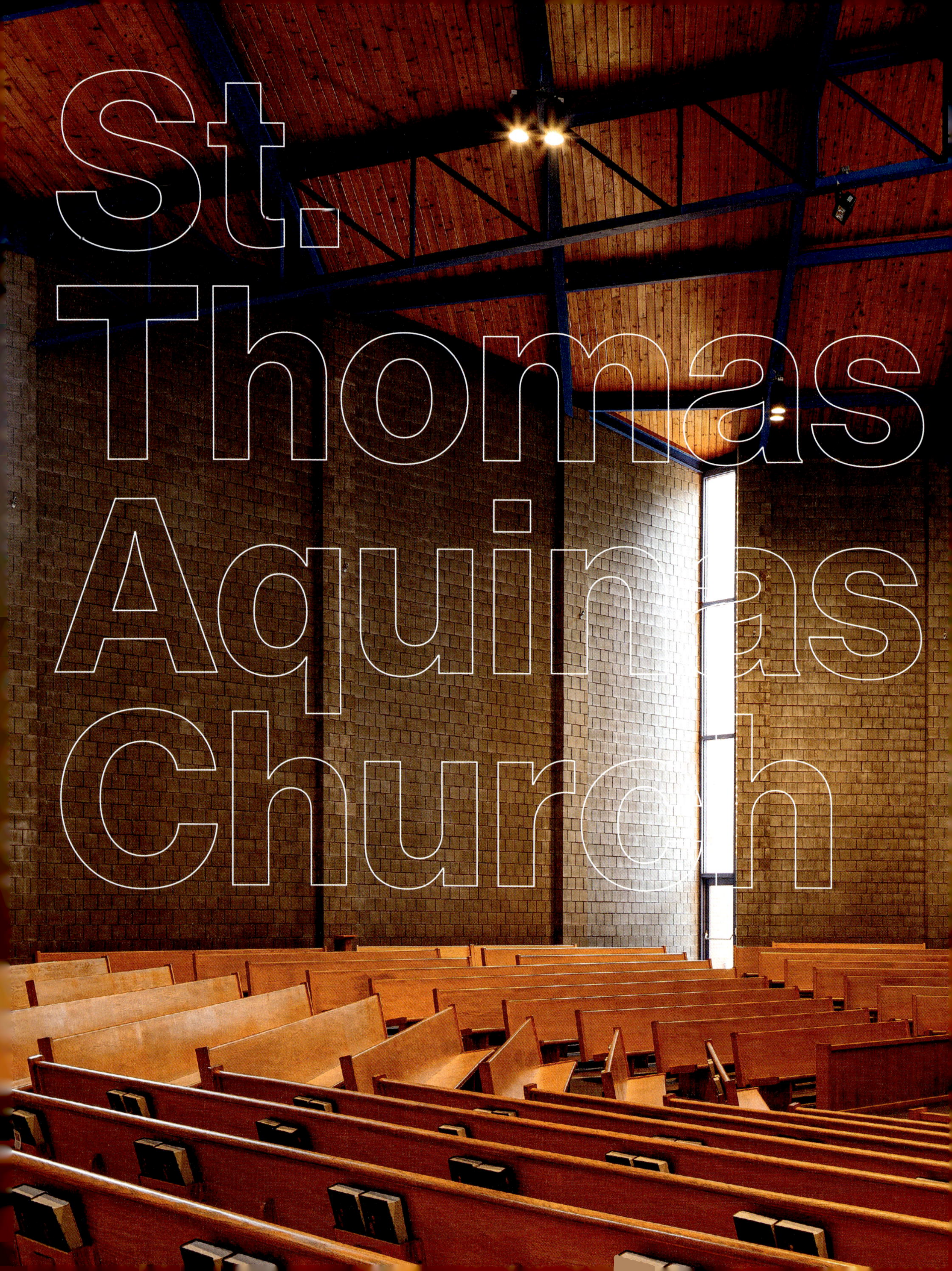

St. Thomas Aquinas Church

St. Thomas Aquinas Church, 1969.

St. Thomas Aquinas Church

1969 | Indianapolis, IN

Religious architecture was an important part of Woollen's career and, at least initially, where he did some of his most boundary-pushing work. As an architect he was intrigued by the spiritual possibilities that churches offered, where ancient ritual and modern design might merge to create a uniquely moving experience for the end user. Their significance transcended the more earthly concerns with which his other projects were usually preoccupied. "Churches are . . . so satisfying because in an unexpressed way one is almost always sure that the people you're working for want something very good in a kind of selfless way," he once told critic Esther McCoy.[1] "And that's inspiring to an architect beyond the desires of a banker or a school superintendent."

St. Thomas Aquinas Church offered such possibilities. Commissioned by a politically progressive Catholic parish on Indianapolis's north side, the new sanctuary building replaced an older wooden structure that had long out served its use.[2] Church leaders gave their architect a tiny budget of $300,000, about a tenth of what was spent on Clowes Memorial Hall. Woollen nonetheless made the most of it, producing an unusual but brilliantly austere design well suited to the more relaxed Catholic services of the 1960s. "We studied pretty carefully what we thought the Second Vatican Council would propose as a new Catholic Liturgy. And we might be responsible for setting a new pattern within the church," Reverend Joseph Dooley, the church's priest, told the *Indianapolis Star*.[3]

Although substantially altered today, the church's original appearance was undeniably avant-garde. There was no steeple or stained-glass windows or grand front steps leading to a large wooden door. Instead, a vaguely trapezoidal mass, mysterious and fortresslike, sat at the far end of a small concrete court that doubled as a parking lot on Sunday mornings. Interceding brick planes composed its geometric and largely windowless facade, giving little indication of what went on inside. If the building was indeed a church, it was missing the usual markers that had defined religious architecture for centuries. "A church is a portrait of its people at a particular moment in time," Woollen was quoted as saying at the building's dedication in 1969.[4] There could be little doubt that St. Thomas was a modern church for a modern congregation.

While the exterior appeared impenetrable, the interior was surprisingly transparent. Entering through a compressed entry portal appended to the building's southeast side, the congregant emerged into a soaring, columnless sanctuary made of plain concrete block. The space was surprisingly well lit; sunlight filtered in from thin, vertical windows hidden between the meeting points of the exterior walls. Overhead a massive, cobalt-blue metal truss supported a ceiling clad in wood planks. Additional bits of exposed plumbing were painted a cheerful canary yellow. Diverging from the familiar cruciform plan of traditional church architecture, rows of pews were fanned around a simple raised altar to form what the firm described as a "liturgical theater" in the style of a bowled amphitheater.[5] On Sundays, mere feet separated Reverend Dooley from his flock. And because there was not a conventional proscenium or altar rail, congregants stood to receive communion rather than knelt.

All these elements bucked years of architectural convention. But the church's most radical feature by far was the thirty-foot-tall cross floating against the altar wall. Designed by staff architect Peter Mayer, the cross's four metal panels formed the

St. Thomas early exterior rendering.

sanctuary's only religious icon, an abstracted crucifix composed by negative space. Its asymmetric design and brilliant, crimson color made an indelible statement – part sculpture, part set design, part shrine. The total effect was pure drama, especially when the piece was illuminated by the perfectly angled spotlight cut out of the church's ceiling. "I don't know how Evans was able to talk the church into accepting it," said Mayer, who fabricated the cross's panels himself at Lynn Molzan's house.[6] Mayer also designed matching stainless steel altar furniture to complete the sanctuary's spare aesthetic. The furniture was modular and removable so the sanctuary could double as a venue for secular concerts when desired.

The St. Thomas project demonstrated several themes that were coming to define Woollen's practice: the choreography of light and color in space; the integration of art, graphics, and furniture within a project's overall design; and, most important, a sincere concern for how a building would affect the people meant to make use of it. Utilizing industrial materials and exposed structures, St. Thomas offered an intentionally raw and unmediated environment for worship. "Cannot the inside be what things are? The outside is slipcovered to please the neighborhood, but on the inside you're face to face with God – or want to be," said Woollen about the project later.[7] By slipcover Woollen meant the red brick that clad the building as opposed to its concrete skeleton left exposed inside the sanctuary. Recalling Louis Kahn's First Unitarian Church of Rochester, Woollen would also employ a similar material palette for a library project at Marian University designed around the same time.

In the broader Midwest, church architecture was a surprising site for architectural experimentation. Like houses, churches proliferated during the postwar building boom, especially in growing suburbia, and modernism flourished among new

***Top left and above*:** Church exterior from street and parking lot, ca. 1969.

***Left*:**
Church exterior as it appeared in 2024. The wraparound addition was added in 2001.

and progressive congregations.[8] Notably, one of the nation's earliest examples of modern church design was also located in Indiana. Designed by Finnish architect Eliel Saarinen and his son, Eero, First Christian Church opened in Columbus, Indiana, in 1942. The building was commissioned by the family of J. Irwin Miller and represented their first foray in architectural patronage. With its gridded facade, totem-esque bell tower, and large reflecting pool, First Christian made national headlines for being both shockingly new and shockingly expensive. "The costliest modern church in the world, planned by Europe's most famous modern architect and his son, is going up across the street from a Victorian city hall and a conventional Carnegie library in Columbus, Ind," *Time* reported as construction was underway.[9] "It is a simply designed church for a simple people," Eliel Saarinen explained to the magazine. Indianapolis residents unable to make the trip down to Columbus could inspect plans for the design themselves when the exhibition *Architectural Designs and Models by Eliel and Eero Saarinen* opened at the John Herron Art Institute that same year.

First Christian Church may have been the most famous modern church in Indiana, if not the country, but it was far from the only one. Other churches across the state, like the triangular sanctuary of Concordia Theological Seminary (1957) in Fort Wayne by Eero Saarinen, the swooping St. Augustine's Episcopal Church (1958) in Gary by Edward D. Dart, or the translucent First Missionary Church (1960) in Berne by Orus Eash, showed just how creative religious architecture could be. In Indianapolis proper there was St. Rita's Catholic

***Above*:**
Sanctuary interior under construction, late 1960s.

***Below*:**
Sanctuary interior, ca. 1969.

Church (1958) by Charles M. Brown and Holy Trinity Hellenic Orthodox Cathedral (1960) by McGuire and Shook Compton, Richey and Associates, both of which featured free-standing slab bell towers and geometric brickwork. Woollen would have also been well acquainted with Christian Theological Seminary (1966), designed by New York architect Edward Larrabee Barnes and funded by Miller's family foundation. Located on thirty-five acres south of Butler University, the complex made an impressive case for the unique potential of modernism in religious architecture, and its spartan yet elegant appearance was well publicized by the press. "Like other architecture that departs from the familiar, [the seminary] will be seen differently by different people and, most likely, it will take a bit of getting used to," reported the *Indianapolis News*.[10]

Like St. Thomas, many of these churches emphasized informality and communal intimacy as a means of heightening one's relationship with God. Their goals were often expressed through the use of simplified forms; raw or unadorned surfaces; and more egalitarian, in-the-round plans. Woollen began his own church architecture career in 1963 with an almost-primitive design for St. Thomas Lutheran Evangelical Church in Bloomington, Indiana, fifty miles south of Indianapolis. Built for $40,000, Woollen likened the church's wooden construction and dramatically pitched roofline to the rustic stave churches of medieval Europe.[11] St. Timothy's Episcopal Church, completed in 1969 on Indianapolis's outskirts, followed a similar model, its exaggerated, angular profile recognizable from all directions. Like St. Thomas, both churches featured centralized plans, a feature increasingly common in modern church architecture by the late 1960s.[12]

The rock-bottom budgets Woollen often contended with were not atypical for small congregations, and more than once did the architect's design ambitions strain what a cash-strapped building committee could feasibly accommodate. A review of Woollen's church designs from the 1960s shows several instances of highly unorthodox, even fanciful schemes that were never completed as planned. For Asbury United Methodist, Woollen imagined a

Model for Asbury United Methodist Church, 1963.

multibuilding campus of Seussian A-frames, with the height of a roof's pitch representing the relative importance of the building's function. For Warren Hills Christian, a young congregation that had previously met in a shopping mall, he envisioned two geometric saucers, each topped with a spire. Perhaps the most elaborate scheme was for King of Glory Lutheran Church, where Woollen proposed a honeycombed plan of hexagonal rooms clustered around a central plaza. Echoing again the work of Kahn, the plan had a "techno-organic" tone rarely seen in Woollen's output.[13] Renderings were published both locally in the *Indianapolis Star* and nationally in *Arts & Architecture* magazine, but when the church finally opened in 1963 its design was considerably toned down.[14] The reason may have been just as much about cost as the radicality of its grandiose design. At the time Lutheran church designs needed to be approved by the denomination's governing body in New York City. Confident in his idea and with the backing of the congregation itself, Woollen traveled there to present his plan, but the scheme was ultimately rejected. The architect took the setback in stride, reasoning that the design's conceptualization and subsequent publication was a reward in and of itself. "I try to take this view of things that all of one's work may not be built," he said. [15] "But it is not a loss. It has a place. It may even be best that all of one's work may not be built."

Except for a freestanding bell tower (Woollen, ever the romantic, referred to it as a *campanile*) originally planned for the church's left flank, St. Thomas came to fruition relatively intact. And if Woollen heard any grumblings from parishioners about the church's bare-boned aesthetic, he kept those critiques to himself. "I can't imagine the priests really liked what we were doing, but I never heard anything about a controversy. But there must have been," Mayer recalled.[16] The project earned positive press coverage locally and nationally, as well as an honor award from the Indiana Society of Architects. But perhaps the most meaningful review came a few years later from Reverend Dooley: "The building looks good only where there are people in it. That says something too, that we don't mind."[17]

Musical Arts Center

Musical Arts Center, ca. 1972.

Musical Arts Center

1972 | Bloomington, IN

The theater on Indiana University's campus went by many names. School administrators, tasked with fundraising millions for the theater's construction, described it as a "laboratory" – a space for education and experimentation as much as performance and spectacle. Others lauded it as "The Met of the Midwest," a world-class opera house rooted, of all places, in the heart of Indiana farm country.[1] Students nicknamed it "Fort Bain" after the IU School of Music's longtime dean, Wilfred C. Bain.[2] But its architect called it "an opera factory."[3] To Woollen it was a place where things were made.

One of the most audacious designs of his entire career, the Musical Arts Center – or the MAC, as the structure was ultimately christened – captured the Brutalist confidence of Woollen's previous work while pushing his practice into new and more mature territory. It allowed Woollen to elaborate further on some of the ideas he and John Johansen had first explored at Clowes Memorial Hall, but this time in full control as the project's lead. For Woollen, now in his late thirties, this was likely freeing but also daunting: the MAC's program was far more complex than Clowes, demanding a highly integrated solution that could satisfy students, faculty, and the public alike. IU leaders envisioned an unusually multipurpose building that would bring together all the parts of opera production – stage, rehearsal space, dance studio, costumery, woodworking shop, and more – under one roof. And, unlike most college theaters, the MAC would be designed specifically for opera. Estimated budgets far exceeded what Woollen had to work with on Clowes, but that didn't mean there would be money to spare. The university initially pegged the project's ideal cost at $10 million but reasoned that only $8 million could be feasibly obtained in the current political and economic climate.[4] By the time the MAC opened in 1972, two years behind schedule, total costs had risen to over $11 million.

There was also the added pressure of what the project meant for IU. As the state's flagship institution of higher learning, the university had grown exponentially in the postwar era, increasing its student population and greatly expanding its campus footprint. The School of Music had also risen in profile, buoyed by prominent faculty appointments and Bain's exacting standards. The school was widely seen as one of the best opera education programs in the country, and its student productions frequently toured nationally.[5] Popular Saturday evening programs welcomed opera lovers (and the opera curious) to Bloomington from all over the Midwest, where they came dressed in "everything from tuxedos to blue jeans," according to one newspaper.[6] The school's current home on campus, East Hall, was a former World War II airplane hangar – laughably unsuited for the needs of a world-class music program. By the early 1960s Bain was planning for its replacement. Over the next decade he would be assisted by two others: Elvis Stahr, IU's president, and Herman B Wells, its chancellor. Wells would passionately lead the MAC's building committee and act as its principal fundraiser, positioning the project at the center of a larger fundraising campaign tied to the university's 1970 sesquicentennial.[7]

Correspondence between Bain, Stahr, and Wells reveals their enthusiasm for the new building's potential as well as their difficulty in raising the required funds. The MAC represented more than just a new building. In the same way that Clowes emblemized Indianapolis's cultural aspirations, so too did the MAC function as a metaphor for the

***Above*:**
Musical Arts Center early exterior rendering used in fundraising materials, 1965. *Courtesy of Indiana University Archives. Rendering by Helmut Jacoby.*

***Below*:**
Illustration for "music workshop and laboratory building" by Eggers and Higgins, 1962. *Courtesy of Indiana University Archives.*

university's – and by proxy, Indiana's – future. Opera was high art. For those who hoped to carve out a more sophisticated reputation for the Hoosier State, opera's continued existence in Indiana, and at the caliber those like Bain demanded, was a cause worth championing. In pitches to potential donors, the trio made clear their ambitions. They routinely compared the MAC's specifications to those of the Metropolitan Opera in New York City, and made sure to mention the multiple trips they took to Europe to tour the renowned opera theaters there for inspiration (including one by Woollen at his own expense). Much attention was also given to the MAC's significance in a region, they said, that was often deprived of first-class cultural offerings. "[The MAC] will provide a constant stream of professionally trained musical talent to vitalize the musical life of Indiana, of America and of the world," Wells and Stahr wrote in a letter to Herman Krannert, the Indianapolis businessman who would ultimately donate $1.85 million to the cause.[8] Other times their appeals were knowingly self-deprecating: "The Midwest is known as a cultural wasteland. There is no reason to accept this criticism without doing something about it," they wrote in a letter to the Cummins Engine Company, whose board would agree to donate $250,000.[9] The other lead gift would come from Columbus's Elsie Irwin Sweeney, the aunt of J. Irwin Miller.[10] A longtime supporter of the School of Music, Sweeney would unfortunately pass away just weeks after the MAC's inauguration.

Woollen was not the first architect to be engaged in the project. Documentation from the time shows that university leaders initially turned to Eggers and Higgins, the New York firm responsible for nearly every building on IU's campus up until that point.[11] Founded by former associates of the Beaux-Art architect John Russell Pope, Eggers and Higgins had done much to establish a grand, Collegiate Gothic idiom for the university's academic buildings. The firm's elegant drawings for a "music workshop and laboratory building," produced in 1962, showed a modern but inoffensive design of descending limestone volumes capped by a round glass lobby.

For reasons that remain unclear, these plans were never adopted. Perhaps Bain and his colleagues were looking for a bolder approach to the commission, or something that would more strongly stress the functional aspects of the new building's program. Or maybe IU's status as a state-funded institution made the selection of an Indiana architect appealing – particularly if that architect had experience, as Woollen did, in theater design. Whatever the reason, by January 1965 Woollen was officially on the job.[12] Wells dashed off a note congratulating the architect on his appointment to the "new Performing Arts Building." The well-wishes came with a challenge: "The function of the building is

Groundbreaking, 1968. Pictured (*from left*) are Elsie Irwin Sweeney, Wilfred Bain, Evans Woollen, and Herman Wells. *Courtesy of Indiana University Archives.*

complex but I am certain that you will find excellent and imaginative solutions. This building is one in which I have long had a keen personal interest so I shall be deeply interested in its development," he wrote.[13] According to one report, Woollen would be the first Hoosier architect to build on IU's campus in three decades.[14]

Woollen once described the MAC as "an automobile or a machine of some kind which you take immediately for what it is and for how it operates and for how it moves and breathes."[15] Large, gray, and boxy, the building was imbued with a vaguely mechanical quality apparent in both its functionalist styling and elemental massing arranged "by necessity, not art." In the modernist tradition, form followed function, and the building's external presentation mirrored the activity that went on inside. Mammoth concrete cylinders, each housing a spiral staircase, anchored the building's four corners like the legs of a table. Between them sat a thick, rectangular plane faced in limestone panels that contained rehearsal spaces and studios. This in turn rested on the MAC's wraparound lobby, formed by a two-story pedestal of glass panes and concrete piers. At the building's summit he placed a shallow semicircular volume, marking the auditorium's interior perimeter, and then another rectangular mass, oblong and turreted, which accommodated its towering fly loft.

The result was a highly varied, composite form – less a single shape and more a conglomerate of geometric building blocks fitted together. It was a structure that rewarded close looking, every angle revealing a new architectural facet or flourish along its rough and striated concrete surfaces. Circles conjoined with squares; curves emptied out into right angles. The design was symmetrical, or almost; only after careful study did one notice the minor differences between the left and right facades, the slight recesses in the frontal fascia, or the slit windows pockmarking the building at irregular intervals. According to Woollen, these eccentricities (reminiscent of another architect known for his work in concrete, Marcel Breuer) were accentuated as the design progressed and made the building "more human and interesting."[16] Indeed an earlier rendering used in fundraising materials showed a

SUMMER MUSIC FESTIVAL
Musical Arts Center
101 North Eagleson Avenue

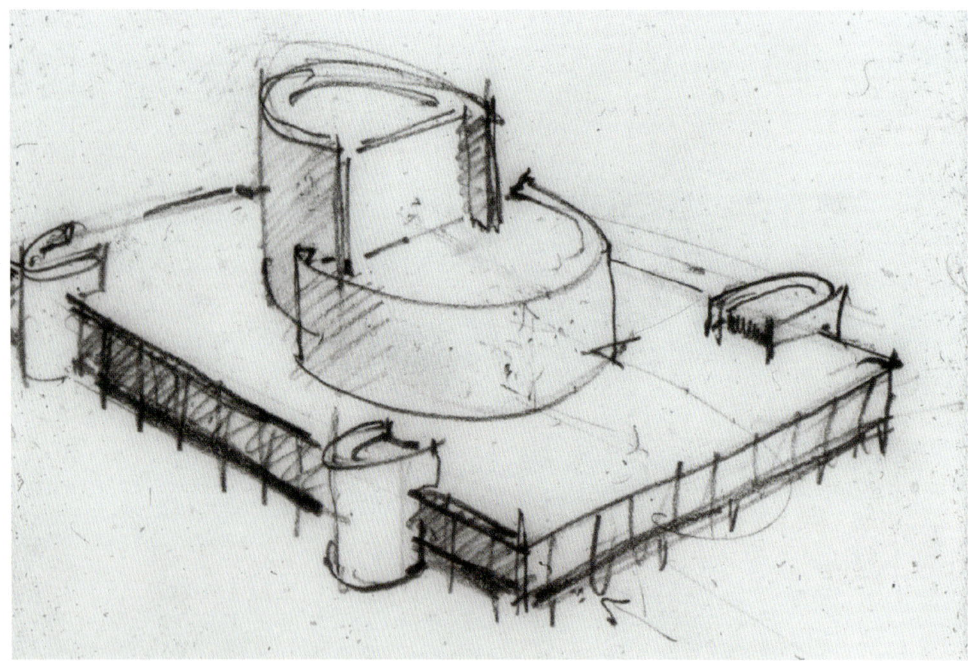

Exploratory sketch, ca. 1965.

Dedication plaque.

more symmetrical building with a central entrance and a long front portico. By the time the building was completed, the entrance had moved to the left side, where it was capped by a shorter concrete awning.

Woollen once referred to himself as "the mad colorist," and no project exhibited Woollen's chromatic inclinations quite like the MAC.[17] If the building's exterior was drab gray, its interior was a surprising cacophony of color. The auditorium featured purple curtains and red plaster walls, so thick and textured they evoked shag carpeting. Above, twinkling gold chandeliers could be raised or lowered for acoustical precision. The space's vibrancy was further intensified by the theater's intentionally small size. To accommodate developing student voices, only eighty feet separated the proscenium from the last row, a noticeable compression of the usual space between audience and performer.

The lobby was even brighter. Here, purple carpeting emblazoned with orange chevrons collided with the building's tough concrete walls. Elevators were orange; upholstered seating banks were blue. Red and white "conversation pits" sat next to mod metal chairs. To Woollen, these seemingly superficial elements were in fact vital contributions to the users' complete spatial experience. "We tried to provide for the psychic needs and for the needs for pleasure as well as the actual needs of function and space. Appearances were a by-product of fulfilling those needs," he told the *Indianapolis News* just before the building's completion.[18]

A program of geometric wall murals, designed by Peter Mayer, was another important aspect of the interior design. Decorating the lobby and adjoining spaces, the murals repeated the square and circle motif found throughout the building. They also served as wayfinding, as in the case of the large *M* and *W* painted on the entrances to the lobby bathrooms. The murals exemplified Woollen's larger interest in "supergraphics," a trend of 1960s and 1970s modern architecture that saw two-dimensional graphic design applied in three-dimensional architectural space. Although little remembered today, the firm's supergraphics would play a starring role in several other projects completed during the 1970s, including Pruis Hall at Ball State University, the A. J. Thatcher Community Center, the Minton-Capehart Federal Building, and the Pilot Center in the Over-the-Rhine neighborhood of Cincinnati.

Woollen was also deeply involved in the selection of artworks to further complement the MAC's Brutalist design, beginning with a monumental sculpture outdoors. Period correspondence reveals that Woollen and campus leaders originally approached the British sculptor Henry Moore for the commission, a choice likely inspired by Moore's previous work at Lincoln Center and, closer to home, the Bartholomew County Public Library in downtown Columbus, Indiana. There Moore delivered an organic bronze arch tall enough to walk under. (As for most of Columbus's artistic treasures, Irwin and Xenia Miller provided the necessary funds for the sculpture's realization.)[19] Planning for the MAC piece appears to have been serious enough that in 1968 Woollen and the art history professor Albert Elsen traveled to London to meet with Moore in person. "We have a superb opportunity to enrich the future history of this university and to become part of what is meaningful in the history of art and architecture," Elsen wrote Wells soon after, arguing strongly for Moore's involvement.[20]

A sculpture by Moore, then one of the world's most famous living artists, would have been an undeniable coup for the MAC. But amid ongoing struggles to fund the building itself, campus leaders soon reasoned that the sculptor's $180,000 fee was "not worth the price – we are simply paying for Moore's name."[21] A more affordable solution was found with another abstract sculptor, Alexander Calder. While perhaps not as prestigious as a Moore bronze, one of Calder's signature steel "stabiles" would still mark the MAC as a place of high culture. Happily, the work could also be painted Calder's signature shade of red – more or less the same color as IU crimson. Produced in France and shipped to Bloomington in pieces, the forty-foot sculpture, titled *Peau Rouge*, was finally erected on the MAC's front lawn in 1971. "That there buildin' with towers, portholes, pieces of crooked iron struck upright in the front yard . . . What's it fer? Opera," quipped the *Sunday Herald-Times* of Bedford, Indiana, referring to Calder's creation in knowingly crude terms.[22]

Art would also have a place inside the theater's lobby in the form of two twenty-by-twenty-foot tapestries created by the artist George Ortman. Like Calder, Ortman was not the team's first choice. The commission was originally given to the Robert Indiana, a native Hoosier artist then living in New York. Renowned for his graphic, text-based paintings and sculptures, Indiana would have brought another degree of art-world celebrity to the venue's profile. Unfortunately, he never completed the commission. In 1970, Woollen wrote to Wells explaining he had visited the artist more than once in New York City and still Indiana had no work to show. Frustrated, Woollen counseled Wells that "it may be time for threatening of cancellation."[23] As the theater's opening loomed, leadership instead pursued Ortman, who had recently joined the faculty of the Cranbrook Institute of Art in Michigan. While it's not clear how the team first encountered Ortman, they may have seen his work at the Indianapolis Museum of Art, where the artist's "construction" paintings were the subject of a recently opened exhibition, or at the Christian Theological Seminary, which counted several Ortman banners as part of its institutional art collection. For the MAC, Ortman delivered two lively felt tapestries in his signature geometric style, as well as a custom flag for the outdoor marquee.

At long last the MAC was officially inaugurated on April 16, 1972. Major newspapers across the country lauded the theater's ambitious program, its bright acoustics, and the space it afforded both students and the public. But reviews of the architecture – and the pop-art interiors – were more ambivalent, and many critics strained to understand the boldness of Woollen's aesthetic choices. The *Indianapolis Star*'s critic thought the building's asymmetrical irregularities gave it a "smart, cocked hat, youthful charm that challenges the observer to expand his idea of what is beautiful."[24] "Clean-lined but sumptuous," declared the *Chicago Tribune*, while the *Boston Globe* thought the auditorium had a "pleasing quality" despite being apparently "designed by a color blind person."[25]

Federal Building

THE SALVATION ARMY
Michigan St
65 70
ONE WAY
ONE WAY

Detail, Federal Building portico and mural, ca. 1976.

Minton-Capehart Federal Building

1974 | Indianapolis, IN

The Minton-Capehart Federal Building has served as a reliable punching bag since its completion in 1974. Likened to everything from a fortress and a bunker to a pigeon coop and an IBM punch card, the building's angled facade – a slanting checkerboard raised up on concrete pilotis – recalled the slope of an Egyptian pyramid or a Mesopotamian ziggurat (albeit in reverse).[1] Critics derided its brash modernity, its Brutalist heft considered unbecoming for the prime location it occupied along one of downtown Indianapolis's main thoroughfares. Dropped with a thud in the heart of the city, its total effect was one of weighty symmetry, colossal and inert. "A monstrosity in concrete," complained one resident to the *Indianapolis Star*.[2] "The building is an ideal design to represent our Federal government – top heavy!" grumbled another to the *Indianapolis News*.[3]

If the Federal Building is Woollen's most hated design, it is also his most misunderstood. "It's not meant to be a pretty building," he would later explain, instead pointing to the office block's larger function within its surrounding spatial environment.[4] The structure's hulking form occupied a full city block along the southeastern edge of the American Legion Mall, a stately but rather desolate open space that extended several blocks along the city's north–south axis. Developed during the City Beautiful movement of the 1920s, the mall was one of Indianapolis's most impressive urban features. Woollen and his staff knew the area well; the firm's offices were located just across the street in a two-story flatiron recognizable by the giant 7UP sign on its roof. Woollen's desk sat in the building's prow, giving him the perfect view from which to study the project and its context. Ringing the mall were several historical landmarks: the Indiana War Memorial, a massive limestone edifice inspired by the Mausoleum of Halicarnassus; the Scottish Rite Cathedral, a neo-Gothic Masonic temple; and the Indianapolis Public Library, a Beaux Arts jewel box designed by architect Paul Philippe Cret (a building for which, some thirty years later, Woollen would design a transformative addition). Immediately facing the building's site was an open plaza with, at its center, a one-hundred-foot-tall black marble obelisk dedicated to the Hoosier casualties of World War I.

As Woollen would explain it, the mall was Indianapolis's version of the great town squares of Italy but lacked any sense of containment or intimacy. What this midwestern piazza needed was not another modernist "tower in the park" office slab – which would have left empty voids around its perimeter – but a bulwark, deliberately horizontal, to define the mall's eastern boundary and create a feeling of enclosure for the pedestrian.[5] It was not a problem Woollen alone could solve – inclusive of the obelisk plaza, the mall stretched from Michigan Street to St. Clair Street, and the Federal Building site controlled only one segment of its border – but at least he could make a start. This new addition, he hoped, would spark "a probably hundred or two hundred year process of enclosing a really remarkably large public space that had no sense of containment."[6] The building's canted "lean" would further the effort (and also echo the pyramidic form of the War Memorial nearby). For additional continuity Woollen specified a buff shade of concrete meant to complement the various limestone facades of the mall's surrounding structures.

The Federal Building was yet another important step forward in Woollen's career. By square footage it was one of the largest public buildings the firm

Aerial view of future Federal Building site, ca. 1964. The intended lot is outlined in yellow.

Illustration of War Memorial Plaza design, ca. 1919, designed by Walker and Weeks. The Indiana War Memorial can be seen in the distance.

had completed to date, and at a cost of $16.7 million, his most expensive. Designed to accommodate two thousand workers from multiple federal agencies, its visibility in the city center would serve as a convincing billboard for the firm's design approach. "A lot of people couldn't stand that Federal Building, but of course I was a young architect just out of school, and I got it. That was the firm that I wanted to be a part of," remembered Christopher Peragine, who joined Woollen, Molzan and Partners in the early 1980s.[7]

The building also arrived at a watershed moment in Indianapolis's postwar maturation. Although technically a project of the US General Services Administration, the federal agency tasked with overseeing the government's vast use of office space, the building's presence – bold, confident, modern, new – in downtown Indianapolis mirrored conversations about the city's civic future unfolding on the local level. The city's recently elected mayor, Republican Richard Lugar, had just orchestrated a sweeping and highly contested consolidation of city and county government called "Unified Government," or Unigov. With the stroke of a pen, Indianapolis became the country's eleventh-largest city (and Lugar its most powerful mayor in history). While Unigov would have many effects, one of the most significant was that the city now qualified for a larger pool of federal grants, and its borrowing limit – a useful tool for financing capital projects in the downtown area – increased.[8] Speaking at the Federal Building's dedication on October 24, 1974, Lugar called for a return to "the concept that local government, state government and Federal government are servants of the people."[9] He went on to describe Woollen's creation as "something beautiful and enduring," a fitting symbol for the Indianapolis of tomorrow.

The Federal Building was one of several heroic concrete government complexes erected in American cities during this time. Emblematic of the "Great Society" ideals espoused by the Kennedy and Johnson presidential administrations, these bold and often aesthetically divisive projects promoted a vision of government that was solid, dignified, and present in public life.[10] Famous Brutalist works like Kallman, McKinnell & Knowles's Boston City Hall (1968) and Curtis & Davis's James V. Forrestal Building in Washington, DC (1969) would have been well-known to Woollen, and one clearly sees their influence in the Federal Building's elongated form, cantilevered floor plates, and gridded fenestration. Woollen also acknowledged the particular influence of Eero Saarinen's American embassy in London, built in 1960.[11] The Federal Building shared the embassy's geometric patterning and blocky massing, with the internal division between first-floor "public" areas and upper-floor offices clearly demarcated in the facade appearance.

Interestingly, exposed concrete does not appear to have been Woollen's first choice for the Federal Building. When the design was first announced in 1967, the local papers described it as a "white modern structure" faced in Indiana limestone, perhaps similar in presentation to Clowes Memorial Hall.[12] At some point during the project's long gestation period while federal funding was being secured, stone was swapped for concrete – a change order likely due to government cost cutting. Raw concrete had an additional, more cynical, function: protection against civil unrest, a concern on the minds of many in the turbulent 1960s and 1970s. "The Feds were very worried about what could happen in the country. We were all concerned with the demonstrations and how the building behaves, so to speak," remembered Erik Sueberkrop, a partner at the time who would later found the internationally known practice STUDIOS in San Francisco.[13]

Seen this way, the Federal Building's raised and imperious facade resembled something like a defensive crouch. To temper this defensiveness, Woollen knew that the building needed something else. A mural, wrapping around the building's loggia, could balance out its oppressive scale and provide a much-needed shot of color to its stoic concrete face. The idea of using art to soften Brutalism's machismo was nothing new, and Woollen himself had leaned on the power of exterior murals several times before. For the A. J. Thatcher Community Center on Indianapolis's far west side, he cheekily emblazoned the words "swim" and "gym" at larger-than-life scale. For the Davlan Apartments, a government-subsidized apartment building the firm renovated a few blocks from the Federal Building's site, he painted a seventy-five-foot-long image of a corncob, its kernels spelling out the word *Hoosier*. Flexible and inexpensive, murals were an ideal strategy for what today might be called "placemaking," imbuing almost any public space with instant personality. Woollen's enthusiasm for these sorts of interventions extended beyond his own projects.

***Above*:**
Mayor Richard Lugar (*center*) at Federal Building dedication ceremony, 1974. Woollen is seated at far right.

***Below*:**
James V. Forrestal Building designed by Curtis and Davis, 1969, Washington, DC.

For instance, he also served on the steering committee for "Urban Walls," a short-lived public arts initiative meant to enliven downtown Indianapolis buildings with artist-designed murals.[14]

The Federal Building's mural was an integral part of Woollen's total vision for the project, and the architect was intimately involved in its creation. In 1973 the General Services Administration convened a blue-ribbon panel to choose an artist who might work on the project. Led by Jan van der Marck, the Dutch-born director of the Museum of Contemporary Art Chicago, the panel – without ever visiting Indianapolis, to Woollen's chagrin – first

salesforce

No Smoking
Beyond This
Point

575
NORTH PENNSYLVANIA

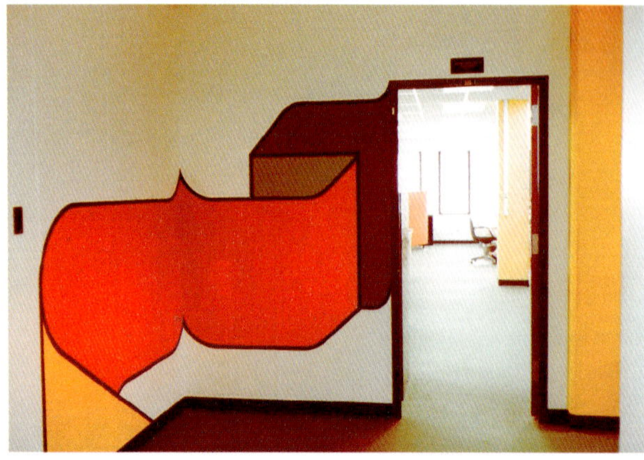

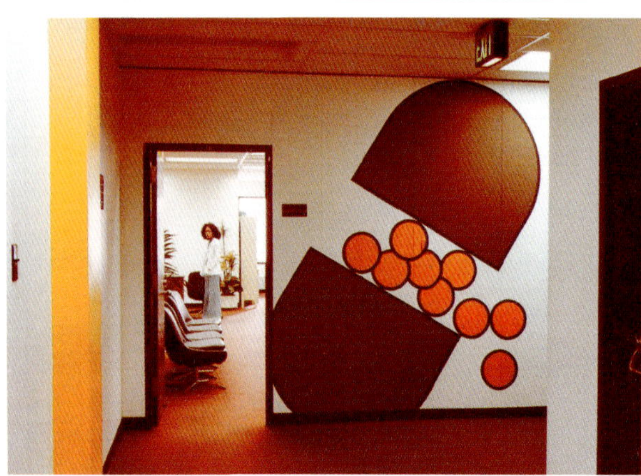

Interior hallway murals, ca. 1975.

proposed the painter Al Held, an abstract expressionist working in New York.[15] Held's selection posed a problem for Woollen. The artist had recently shifted to only painting in black and white, and Woollen felt such a dour palette would run counter to the mural's intended purpose. Thus an anti-Held was procured: designer Milton Glaser. Today Glaser is recognized as one of the foremost graphic designers of the twentieth century, famous for creating the iconic "I Love New York" logo in 1976. But in 1973 he was most known for his editorial work, a pop art illustrator with a psychedelic, sometimes irreverent style. Unlike Held, he was not a blue-chip "fine artist." He had far more experience working at the scale of a concert poster or a magazine spread (he had helped found *New York Magazine* a few years prior) than that of a wall-sized mural. Nonetheless Glaser's wizardry with color, plus his general enthusiasm for the project, would prove him to be the perfect choice.

After studying the site and discussing the project's goals with Woollen, Glaser proposed *Color Fuses*, a contiguous, 672-foot mural of thirty-five different hues – a "continuous Rothko," as Woollen put it.[16] Like a rainbow, each color would bleed imperceptibly into the next. The whole plan was conceptually simple but technically complex to produce, and it broke sharply with the designer's usual figurative style.[17] It would take an Indianapolis paint crew seven months to complete. "I tried to create a non-figurative element that would express a sort of friendly invitation to a building that is necessarily quite formal in its architecture," said Glaser, who was paid $75,000 for his work.[18] He also specified a custom lighting scheme that would pulsate across the mural's length in two minute cycles.

Glaser's mural would prove to be every bit as polarizing as Woollen's architecture. As the building neared completion, the *Indianapolis Star* reported that guffawing motorists, distracted by the twenty-seven-foot-high colored panels going up, were drifting into one another's lanes.[19] Residents of the nearby Riley Center also complained about the blinking lights; the system was turned off after a few months to save energy.[20] To Woollen, all these critiques seemed to misunderstand the point. "[*Color*

Milton Glaser, 1974.

Fuses] wishes to be a billboard of happiness – unless the recipient happens to fear color," he later said.[21] The mural languished for decades until a comprehensive restoration by the General Service Administration in 2012 returned Glaser's design to its original vibrancy. As part of that effort, the special pulsating lighting scheme was also restored.

According to Woollen, painted murals brought a welcome dose of "wit" to the seriousness of architecture. "You can feel intimidated by a building or loosen up because the building is telling you to," he said.[22] While largely forgotten today, murals were also brought inside the Federal Building in the form of twenty geometric supergraphics that decorated various interior corridors and entryways. The graphics were designed by staff architect James McQuiston and, although separate from Glaser's own artistic intervention, they brought a similarly vibrant energy to what was effectively the bureaucratic innards of a governmental office block. For the building's cafeteria, McQuiston also designed a large wall-mounted photomontage depicting scenes from Indianapolis's history.

The Federal Building was one of Woollen's last truly Brutalist designs. It was also one of his last to feature murals or supergraphics. In the years following, the architect's work would move into a noticeably different territory – one that was less bombastic; more subtle; and strongly tempered by an ever-increasing awareness of the relationships between building, environment, and user. As the *Indianapolis Star Magazine* reported in 1976, "The weakness of [Woollen's] earlier architecture, he explains, is that there was too much of his own ego injected into the work and not enough attention to the environment where the building was to be constructed."[23] It would be unfair to say that Woollen *completely* ignored the Federal Building's context; in fact, its surroundings were one of the primary influences on the building's design. But if the Federal Building's heavy form and hard exterior were *meant* as a handshake with the wider world, Woollen would ensure such intentions were made far more explicit in the future.

New Harmony Inn
Registration

New Harmony Inn, showing dormitory (*foreground*) and entry house (*background*), ca. 1975.

New Harmony Inn

1975 | New Harmony, IN

New Harmony, Indiana – population less than one thousand – is just a speck of a town, pinned to the banks of the Wabash River as it meanders along the state's southwestern edge. Surrounded by farmland and wide-open sky, the town feels like a place out of time, as if yanked from the slipstream that stretches from Indiana's agrarian past to its urbanized present.

New Harmony's story began in 1814, when a group of German religious refugees, known as the Harmony Society, settled the area to wait for the Second Coming of Christ. Industrious and egalitarian, the Harmonists laid out a rationally gridded urban plan and populated it with simple log, brick, and wooden structures. Complete with a textile mill, distillery, and acres of vineyards and orchards, New Harmony represented a utopia of its inhabitants' own design.[1] The town graveyard had no headstones; in the Harmonists' eyes, all people were equal in both life and death.

The Harmonist experiment lasted only ten years, but the town's idyllic character and vernacular architecture were preserved more than a century later thanks to the efforts of Jane Blaffer Owen, a Texas-born oil heiress whose husband's ancestor, the social reformer Robert Owen, had purchased the town from the Harmonists in 1825. Beginning in the 1950s, Owen committed millions to restoring the homes, meeting halls, and storehouses the Harmonists had left behind. Woollen was familiar with New Harmony from boyhood visits with his family, yet Owen's vision for this tucked-away corner of the state represented something new and profound.[2] Invited by Owen to design New Harmony's first proper hotel, Woollen recognized the gravity of the assignment. "It was as though a bell jar had been put over the town," Woollen said, "and with the Inn we did not want to let too much air in."[3]

Woollen completed multiple projects over the years for Owen, but the inn was their most significant collaboration. A woman of eclectic interests and the wealth to pursue them, Owen envisioned a new chapter for New Harmony as a national center for spiritual education, dialogue, and convening. The forty-five-room inn would provide much-needed lodging for tourists while also inaugurating them in the distinctive ethos Owen was imagining. "I want this [hotel] just to be a place where people can escape the polluted air of the city and come here and relax and meditate," she told one local paper.[4] The project also complemented another Owen enterprise next door, the Red Geranium Restaurant, for which Woollen designed a small addition in 1968.

To Woollen, Owen's support likely felt like an important form of recognition. It linked him to several other prominent architects and artists – Frederick Kiesler, Jacques Lipchitz, James Rosati, and, later, Richard Meier – whom Owen also engaged for projects in town. While often overshadowed by J. Irwin Miller in Columbus, Owen's patronage of modern design was significant and multifaceted.[5] One of her closest collaborators was someone Woollen also knew: Philip Johnson. In 1956 Owen approached Johnson with the idea to build what she described as "an altar that was not an altar and a church that was not a church" for New Harmony.[6] His solution was an undulating, open-air pavilion, covered in shingles and set like a jewel in a walled limestone court. (Owen would later call on Woollen to replace this court, which became too hot to walk on during summertime, with a grassy lawn and central path.)[7] Dubbed the Roofless Church, its idiosyncratic design garnered much attention for New Harmony and Owen's activities there. Its form was an unusual one for Johnson, rich in historical and contextual allusions. Above all, it exemplified his patron's vision for New Harmony at the intersection of past and present, tradition and modernity.[8] The inn would follow a similar path.

Up until this point, Woollen had been a serial modernist, and explicit historical references were not part of his normal vocabulary. He blamed this tendency on his formative experiences as a young designer educated during the apogee of International Style modernism in the United States. "I had some classicist leanings from early professional times, but they were just not encouraged. I consider Mies [van der Rohe], [Philip] Johnson, and [Louis] Kahn to be 'modern classicists,' and circumstances and disposition drew me to them. I continued practicing as a modernist through the '60s," he once reflected to an interviewer.[9] Still, close observers of the architect's output would have noticed a reverence for the past unusual among modernists of his generation. He often looked to historic architecture for inspiration, and even when working in an expressly contemporary idiom, his buildings almost always made subtle yet empathetic gestures to older structures that surrounded them. He was also known as a vocal proponent of historical preservation in downtown Indianapolis. For an *Architectural Record* article about his work published in 1967, nearly a decade before the inn's completion, Woollen laid out his point of view: "We collaborate with the past and the present; we thrive on the continuing argument and opposition about us. We need help; we are not alone, but are – at best – involved."[10]

The architect's initial proposal for the inn, produced sometime during the late 1960s, looked like one of his typical creations of this period. Squat, muscular, and less than hospitable, the angular design had all the trappings of a Woollen building yet nearly nothing in common with New Harmony's historic character. When the desired land for the project could not be acquired, the design was ultimately abandoned – a blessing in disguise. "I am very happy it was never built," Woollen later told a local newspaper.[11] Woollen went back to the drawing board and returned with a revised design that signaled a foundationally different approach. Gone were the chunky massing and Corbusian overhangs. The program now consisted of two separate

Model of initial inn design, ca. 1969.

Above:
The Roofless Church by Philip Johnson, 1960.

Below:
Aerial view of New Harmony Inn (*upper right*) and Roofless Church (*lower left*).

structures: a small, street-facing building known in New Harmony parlance as the "entry house," and a larger hotel block, called the "dormitory." Both were gabled and made of brick. They were sited on a large open lot on North Street, a convenient location for out-of-town visitors and, most important, right across the street from the Roofless Church.

The inn's proximity to the Roofless Church must have felt like a symbolic reunion for Woollen with his former teacher and employer, and the inn's plan clearly acknowledged this relationship. For instance, the dormitory's east–west orientation pointed directly toward the massive gates of the church's forecourt. The two sites were connected by a private alleyway bordering the Red Geranium and Tillich Park, another Owen-sponsored project, designed by Johnson and the landscape architecture firm Zion & Breen.

Checking in for the first time, hotel guests may have been struck by the bare simplicity of Woollen's design. Both the entry house and the dormitory were straightforward structures with shake roofs and expressed chimneys, obviously reminiscent of the historic Harmonist architecture around town. No raw concrete or colorful supergraphics could be found; instead, Woollen wove a contemporary sensibility directly into the massing of the building's elemental forms. On the dormitory's north side, cascading geometric setbacks created a series of balconies and broke up an otherwise flat facade. Asymmetric windows of various sizes enlivened the east and west ends, an effect Woollen likened to a Christmas advent calendar.[12] Like an abstract send-up of American vernacular architecture, the overall result was a crisp and surprising mosaic of planar geometries, old and new. A manicured lawn, crisscrossed by foot paths, connected the dormitory to the entry house and a small pond on property. Owen believed a connection to nature was vital for spiritual enlightenment, and the inn's landscaping was meticulously maintained by an army of groundskeepers.

The dormitory's interiors were another canvas for Woollen to play with. Rooms were minimally furnished with few frills or luxury conveniences. There were no TVs, but many rooms had fireplaces, and

ROSEBANK
—WEST—
111-116
211-216
300-316

NEITHER SHALL YOU

HONOUR YOUR FATHER
AND YOUR MOTHER

OBSERVE THE SABBATH DAY
TO KEEP IT HOLY

The Atheneum, designed by Richard Meier and Partners, 1979.

the larger suites included sleeping lofts reachable by a spiral staircase (a Woollen favorite).[13] Woollen and his staff designed much of the furniture, which was built out of yellow poplar in the Harmonist tradition. Other pieces, like the modernist rattan chairs imported from Italy, furthered the period feeling through a stylish, contemporary filter.

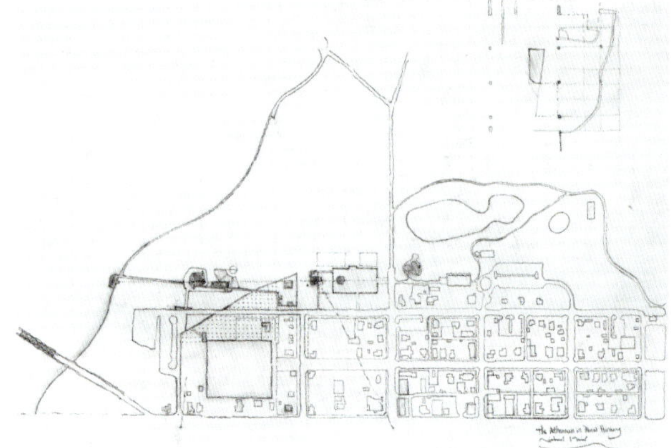

New Harmony town plan drawn by Richard Meier, 1975.

The entry house showed the same savvy restraint. Its most distinctive feature, a holdover from the inn's first design, was a small, cylindrical prayer chapel appended to the building's rear.[14] Exterior stone plaques, inscribed by renowned letter cutter Ralph Beyer with the words of the Ten Commandments, marked the silo as a sacred space. Inside, the room was bare except for a minimalist altar and a few crucifixes. A skylight cast dramatic shadows on the chapel's curved white walls and dark, block wood floor. Woollen had played extensively with the contrast between round and square, blunt and sharp, at the Musical Arts Center, but here the effect was far more intimate and evocative. The chapel's resemblance to a silo or grain elevator made sense given its setting in southern Indiana farm country. The architect may have also been aware of the American silo's significance to the history of European modernism, where it had served as unlikely inspiration for designers like Le Corbusier and Walter Gropius since the 1910s.[15] Synthesizing these precedents for his own purposes, Woollen transformed what had been originally received as an icon of industrialization into something far softer and human scaled. The silo form would show up again and again in subsequent projects.

The inn was completed in 1975. Glimpsed among the clapboard houses and picket fences lining North Street, it likely barely registered as "modern" architecture at all. Some wondered whether Woollen was sublimating himself too much: "In being so modest, so particular to the place, is [the New Harmony Inn] being particular to itself (presuming, as architects usually do, that buildings are each meant in some way to be quite special)?" asked the critic Gerald Allen in his largely positive review for *Architectural Record*.[16] This modesty would only be amplified by the arrival, four years later, of another contemporary building in New Harmony, the Atheneum visitor's center by New York architect Richard Meier. The Atheneum was not personally funded by Owen – its financing came from private foundations – but it completed her vision for New Harmony's rejuvenation, and Meier was expressly chosen in hopes of the monumental "gateway" he might build.[17] The hypercontemporary structure ("Janes' folly," as it was allegedly called by locals) was everything the inn was not.[18] Complexly rendered and blazingly white, less than a half mile separated the Atheneum from the inn, but philosophically the two projects were worlds apart.[19] With the inn Woollen referenced context overtly through material and shape. Meier's approach was far more implied, suggested primarily by his building's axial orientation toward river and town.[20] As he was developing the design, Meier produced a hand-drawn map of New Harmony demonstrating the logic of the Atheneum's positioning. He drew a straight dotted line from the Atheneum to the Roofless Church, perfectly bisecting Johnson's walled court. Had the line continued, it would have naturally terminated at the inn as well.

The inn was a watershed in Woollen's practice. Historically minded and rooted in place, it quietly declared a radical turn in the way Woollen thought about architecture. The project was an early demonstration of what he called situational architecture, a philosophy that would dominate his design approach in the ensuing decades. In a 1994 documentary about his work (funded, in part, by Owen), the architect reflected on how the inn's "situation" in New Harmony informed its design: "It's what people have built, and what they have left in terms of their thoughts and meanings that tell us what to build," he said.[21] This contrasted with what he called "a very different and possibly valid approach that Richard Meier took in the Atheneum, where a beautiful, very white building has been parachuted in and placed at the very edge of New Harmony." With the New Harmony Inn, Woollen decided he was no parachuter. Situationalism – in form, tone, and meaning – would define all of his work to come.

M

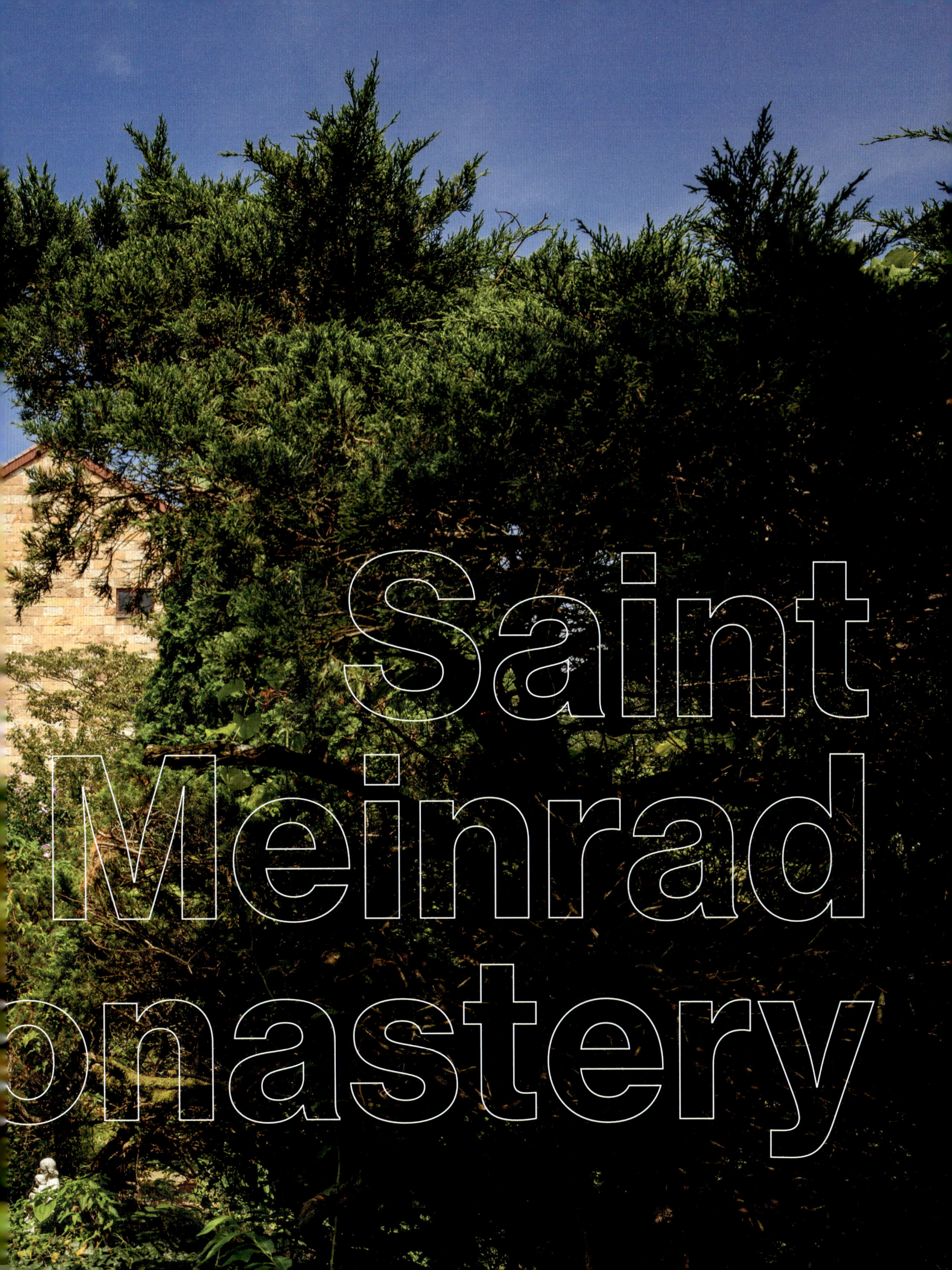
Saint
Meinrad
onastery

Aerial view of Saint Meinrad Monastery, ca. 1982.

Saint Meinrad Monastery

1982 | Saint Meinrad, IN

Architecture by consensus is a difficult proposition. Ask a hundred people how a building should work, and you are bound to receive a hundred different, and likely contradictory, proposals. The best location, the smartest layout, the most pleasing design: in architecture these are personal, even emotional decisions. Professional architects – or at least those in the service of paying clients – know this conundrum well. Father Gavin Barnes of Saint Meinrad Archabbey was discovering it for the first time.

As a Benedictine monk, Barnes had little experience with building construction. He was a theologian with a master's degree from Northwestern University, more at home in the seminary classroom or running Saint Meinrad's extracurricular theater program. But he had spent most of his life on Saint Meinrad's hilltop campus in southern Indiana, embracing the order's ancient philosophy of *ora et labora:* pray and work. Now nearing his fiftieth birthday, Barnes knew Saint Meinrad better than most. So when the abbot asked Barnes to lead the construction of a new monastery building – an expensive undertaking for any institution – he also knew his *confreres*, or fellow monks, would have plenty of opinions about their new home.

The monks were more than happy to share, as the records of their requests (fastidiously preserved in Saint Meinrad's archives) show. Brother Samuel said he was looking for absolute simplicity, with "paint and plaster" kept to a minimum. Father Killian wanted a quiet building; the current monastery, which the monks had lived in continuously since 1874, was much too loud. Brother Paschal agreed: "No flushing toilets, no stereo, TV, or radio sounds," he suggested in a handwritten note. Father Maurus drew out a diagram visualizing how rooms should be arranged. Father Eric was dubious of the need for air-conditioning. People around the world lived without it; why shouldn't the monks? Brother Benedict was not convinced a new building was necessary at all.[1]

Unfortunately for Brother Benedict, the $7.5 million project was already in motion. A construction firm was on board, and Woollen had been tapped as the designer. Woollen's selection seems to have been influenced by two factors. First, the monks were aware of Jane Owen's work in New Harmony and had admired the contemporary but restrained aesthetic Woollen had brought to the New Harmony Inn. Second, he came recommended by another midwestern abbey, St. Procopius in Lisle, Illinois, which had earlier completed its own building project in the Brutalist style. While St. Procopius had ultimately worked with the architect Edward Dart, its leadership suggested Saint Meinrad consider designers such as "Evan Woollens," Harry Weese, or the firm Booth & Nagle, and to visit Columbus, Indiana, for additional inspiration.[2] After interviewing multiple candidates, the abbot posted his decision on the monastery bulletin board: Woollen had won the project.

The opportunity to design a monastery is exceedingly rare for any architect. Founded in 1854 by Swiss missionaries, Saint Meinrad is one of only two Benedictine archabbeys in the United States and one of eleven in the world. For Woollen it must have been an unexpected but exciting challenge, and one tailor-made to his interests. He had deep experience in church design, and his work in New Harmony had exposed him to a broad form of spiritualism that imbued all aspects of the physical environment. The sheer scale of the Saint Meinrad commission was no doubt alluring too, a massive canvas on which to create a work of architectural significance. While Woollen's approach would be very different, it is hard to think that famous modern monasteries like Le Corbusier's Sainte Marie de La Tourette in Lyon or Marcel Breuer's Saint John's Abbey in Minnesota were not far from his mind.

The Saint Meinrad campus was more than just a collection of buildings; it was a self-contained ecosystem of communal life, religious education, and cottage industry. In addition to the seminary, the monks operated a four-year college as well as several small businesses, including a butcher shop, printing press, and coffin workshop. Imposing stone edifices stood side by side with humble farmhouses and clapboard sheds. But the new monastery building would be one of the most important structures on-site, second only to Saint Meinrad's Romanesque Revival church whose twin spires soared over the entire area. The church was where the monks prayed, but the monastery was where they lived. They described it to Woollen as nothing less than "a house of God."[3]

One of the more unusual aspects of the project was the monks' explicit demand for privacy. A monastery's very purpose is to physically remove its inhabitants from the rest of the world. Quiet is the point. Therefore, most of the project's square footage would need to be "cloistered" – off-limits to anyone outside the Saint Meinrad community. For Woollen it was likely an intriguing paradox. The architect was used to designing highly public buildings. His work enjoyed broad visibility, and public exposure was not only expected but usually prized. Never before had a client asked for architecture to be purposefully hidden from view. What would it mean to design not for the masses but for only the select few?

To truly understand this unique brief, Woollen made the radical decision to live among the monks on Saint Meinrad's campus for two weeks. There, he observed for himself his clients' highly structured daily schedule, known as the *horarium*. Days started at 5:30 a.m. with prayer and ended in the evening with more prayer, personal reflection, and study. "We didn't put him up in the guest quarters. We let him live right in the midst of us," Barnes later remembered, a testament to the monks' comfort with Woollen's outsider presence.[4]

This experience, as well as a two-month tour Woollen completed of monastic architecture across Europe, informed much of the building's design. Woollen conceived of the monastery proper as a "passive fortress" in the form of a three-story triangle surrounding a large central courtyard.[5] The scheme was rich in symbolism, pointing both to the image of the Holy Trinity as well as an ecumenical village ringing a town square. Repeated arched windows mimicked the rhythm of a medieval arcade. Woollen specified the entire building be clad in a beige-colored stone known locally as Saint Meinrad sandstone, a material historically quarried by the monks themselves. However, funding could only be secured to cover the monastery's exterior in stone, leaving interior walls bare. In Woollen's usual way, he spun this hiccup into a "happy limitation," rationalizing that "the inside of the large cloister court could then be a smooth creamy white plaster, the soft underbelly of the building as it were."[6]

There were more metaphors. At the triangle's vertices Woollen positioned three large, rectilinear masses, each an allegorical portal for monastic life: one to the public, one to the world, and one to the church. The triangle's western point was the portal to the public, a near-symmetrical facade distinguished by a gabled roofline and a massive wooden door. Simple limestone columns and a radial lunette window bridged the medieval with the modern, as did an inlaid cornerstone inscribed with the word *Pax* and two dates: 480, the year Saint Benedict was born, and 1980, the year the monastery's construction began – situating Woollen's creation within more than a thousand years of monastic tradition.

The triangle's far east vertex – the portal to the world – also linked past with present. Here Woollen inserted a dramatic, neo-Palladian belvedere that offered the monks their own private viewing platform of the surrounding Anderson River valley. Puncturing the courtyard's walled serenity, the twenty-six-foot-tall opening was yet another evocation of the monk's existence at Saint Meinrad, both of the world and apart from it.

The third and final mass, abutting the archabbey sanctuary itself, was the portal to the church. Here Woollen positioned an additional structure called the refectory. This was the monks' eating hall, and Woollen paid this important space special consideration. Its placement next to the church was an allusion to the necessity of both spiritual and bodily nourishment. In a program of primarily rectangular forms, the refectory was octagonal, with large windows and an open floor plan. Hidden skylights, tucked along the ceiling's edges, made the roof appear like it was hovering in place. The room's drumlike form and conical top recalled the medieval chapter houses, or meeting rooms, Woollen had seen on his European tour. Those familiar with the architect's previous work would have also noted the structure's similarities to earlier in-the-round designs, such as the Leibman house, St. Thomas Lutheran Evangelical Church, or St. Richard's Episcopal School (a project ultimately completed sans polygonic wing).

Despite the refectory's expressiveness, Woollen was mindful of the monks' overall commitment to austerity. No fancy features, no superfluous details. "I think that the community is basically conservative, in the sense of not wanting much excess or luxury in the new monastery. We are used to living in an old building where convenience is at a minimum. This we should try to keep," one monk wrote to Barnes.[7] While other clients may have jumped at the possibility of formal innovation or aesthetic flourishes, the monks wanted the exact opposite. Unsurprisingly, this led to unique conversations between Woollen and his team. Small details that might have been a foregone conclusion in any normal project – for instance, whether the monks could have carpeting in their bedrooms – became existential questions. "My greatest victory was convincing [Woollen] to get rid of the carpet on the first floor. This was just me invoking the Trappist along the river. And what were Benedictines doing getting so soft?" remembered Christopher Peragine, a staff architect who worked on the project and spent considerable time on-site.[8]

Such desires not only aligned with Woollen's increasing suspicion of egotistical architectural

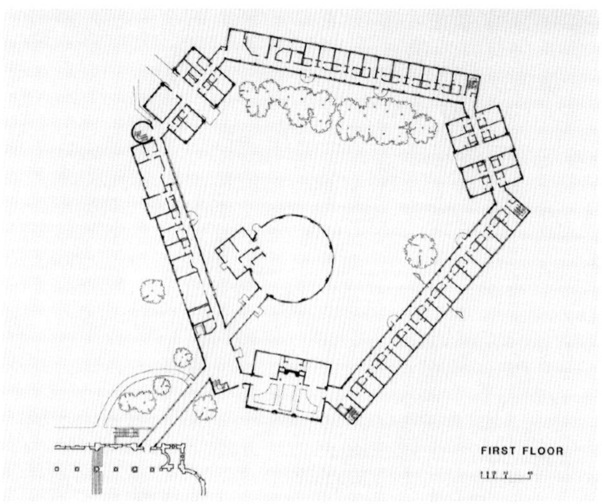

***Above*:**
Interior courtyard, 1982.

***Below*:**
Floor plan.

Interior courtyard, facing the refectory (*foreground*) and Archabbey Church (*background*), 1982.

manifestos; it made sublimation a defining feature of the design's conceit. Yet as the refectory proved, this did not prevent the building from being beautiful in its own restrained way. "There was no doubt he was about the aesthetics of things," explained Father Harry Hagan, a soft-spoken monk who interacted with Woollen during the monastery project as well as a later restoration of the archabbey's sanctuary. "We knew he was someone building in a sort of Shaker aesthetic that would appeal to us. It wasn't just utilitarian," he said.[9] After much internal discussion, the monks did settle on two worldly indulgences: air-conditioning throughout the monastery, and a private bathroom for each cell.

The world today looks very different than it did when Woollen first set foot on Saint Meinrad's campus. Since the monastery was completed, the monks' membership has declined. The college has closed, as have many of the archabbey's businesses. To accommodate the community's aging population, a small expansion was made to the monastery's infirmary, which also necessitated walling off the open belvedere. A nondescript library building, designed by Woollen at the same time as the monastery, has also been altered significantly thanks to a perpetually leaky roof.

But despite these modifications, the complex still stands as Woollen, Barnes, and the Saint Meinrad community originally conceived of it: a functional monument to devotional life. In this sense the building continues to do its job. Every day the monks of Saint Meinrad rise before dawn, just as they have for centuries. They assemble in the church for prayer and in the refectory for fellowship. They tend to the grounds, clean the corridors, cook meals, and minister to visitors. *Ora et labora*. Three decades later Hagan deemed the building – so far – a success. "We don't talk about it really. I guess that means it works," he said.[10]

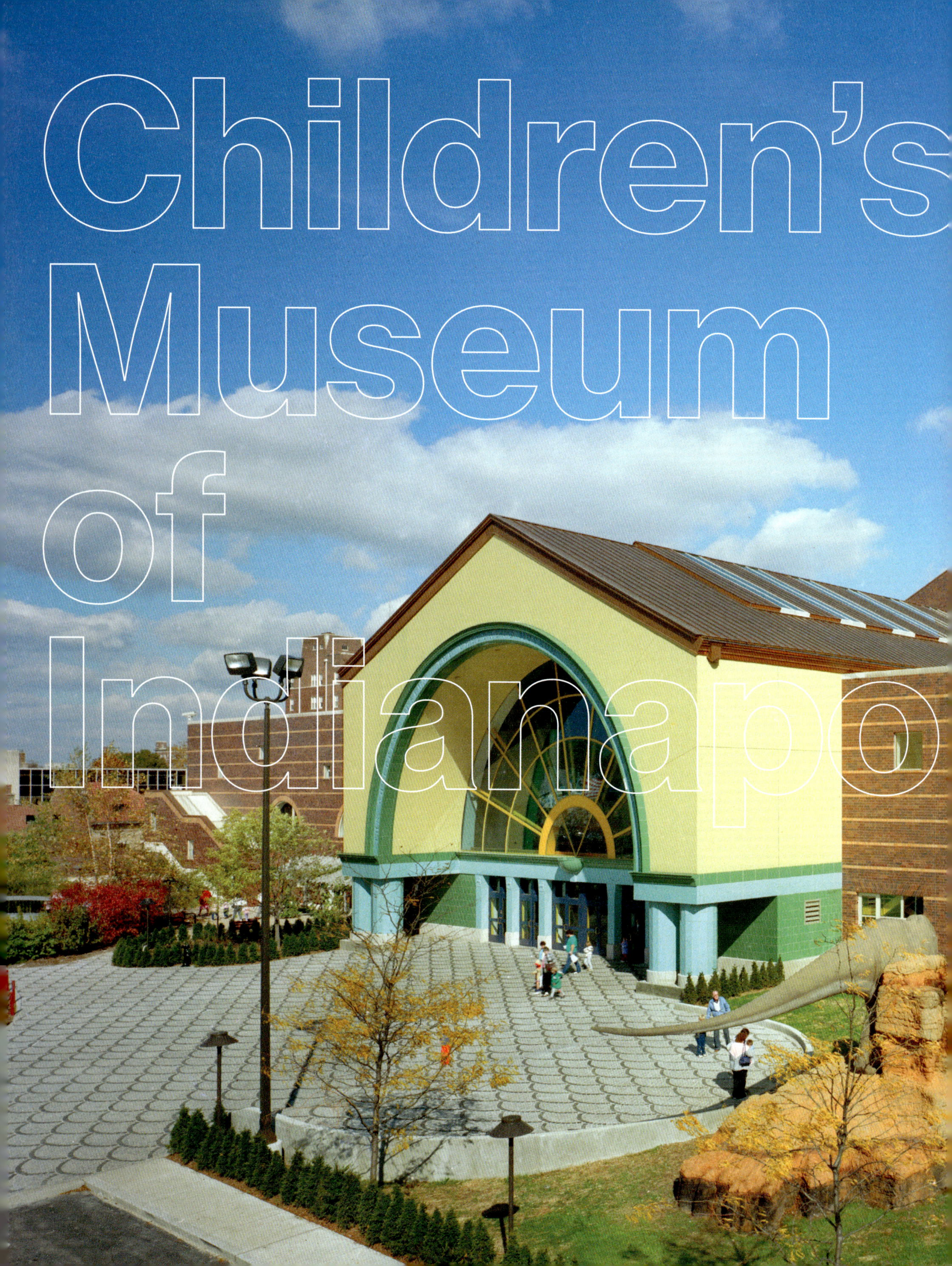

Children's Museum of Indianapo

Children's Museum of Indianapolis, 1989.

Children's Museum of Indianapolis

1989 | Indianapolis, IN

The Children's Museum of Indianapolis remains one of Woollen's most enduringly recognizable projects. A highly visited piece of cultural infrastructure wrapped up in a colorful and iconic package, the project extended the architect's run of important civic commissions following the heightened success of his practice during the 1960s and 1970s. Upon its completion in 1989, Woollen could now boast he had designed not one but two of Indianapolis's landmark cultural institutions: the Children's Museum and Clowes Memorial Hall. Ironically, the two buildings looked nothing alike. Their differences exemplified the changes Woollen's architecture had undergone in the nearly thirty-year gulf between them.

Woollen's city had also changed, and the Children's Museum belonged to its next phase. In the 1950s and 1960s, urban renewal efforts were focused on shoring up Indianapolis's basic infrastructure. Yet no new highway or apartment tower could fix what local leaders saw by the 1970s as an even more intractable problem: the city was boring. "While the city has changed greatly during the last decade, there is little evidence that its image has changed," conceded a report commissioned by the Indianapolis Chamber of Commerce in 1972.[1] St. Louis had the Gateway Arch and Detroit had Greenfield Village. What did Indianapolis have? According to the report's authors, there was the Indianapolis 500 . . . and not much else. "Unlike a major cultural or education institution, an automobile race does not strongly convey a positive impression of the quality of life in a community," the report stated plainly.

The city's impulse toward self-improvement went into overdrive, with sports, tourism, and cultural cachet identified as key areas of focus. In addition to the Children's Museum, a raft of cultural amenities – the Indianapolis Zoo, Indianapolis Museum of Art, Eiteljorg Museum of American Indians and Western Art, City Market, Pan American Plaza, and National Institute for Fitness and Sport among them – were either built, expanded, or renovated during this time. Hotels and office towers, taller and more elaborate than those of the previous decades, sprouted up all over town. Older structures were restored, like the Indiana Repertory Theatre and Union Station, two historic renovations projects to which Woollen's firm contributed. In 1983 residents watched the inflatable roof of their city's new NFL stadium fill with air for the first time. Never mind that no team was (yet) secured to play there: big things were happening, and Indianapolis was determined to leave the stereotype of "Indianoplace" behind. "Move over New York. Apple is our middle name," declared the city's visitor's bureau.[2]

The Children's Museum was Woollen's signature work of this era, but he also played a lesser-known role in Indianapolis's growth in other ways. In partnership with the Pittsburgh-based architect and urban design pioneer David Lewis, Woollen produced the first long-range master plan for IUPUI, the combined Indianapolis campus of Indiana University and Purdue University being built west of the central business district. Planning toward a great urban university in Indianapolis had been ongoing for years, and the idea of a dedicated "University Quarter" was a key part of the city's long-term vision.[3] Woollen and Lewis's proposal, presented in 1975, imagined a bucolic campus dotted by twenty-two new buildings and – most unusually – a nine-block elevated walkway running through it like a "spine." The so-called spine would improve connectivity while also providing IUPUI with, as their report noted, "an 'identity' somewhat unique and much

Woollen (*seated at left*) presenting IUPUI master plan, 1975.

desired."[4] The Pollyanna plan was never adopted, instead absorbed into a later master planning exercise conducted by Edward Larrabee Barnes, who would build several buildings on campus.[5]

Woollen and Lewis also worked together on what was probably Indianapolis's most ambitious cultural project of this era, White River Park. A 250-acre leisure district situated next door to IUPUI, the project was hailed as Indianapolis's own version of Tivoli Gardens. In 1980 the two helped organize a four-day brainstorm to develop the park's very first design concept. Holed up in a downtown hotel, national figures like the urban planner Kevin Lynch, the leader of Central Park's revitalization Elizabeth Barlow Rogers, and the landscape architect Robert Hanna joined Woollen in imagining a waterfront park "focused on food and life, a concept that grows naturally out of Indiana's preeminence in agriculture, sports and medicine."[6] The group's final report articulated many of the ideas later taken up by the city's selected master planning team, a star-studded coalition that included the firm Howard, Needles, Tammen & Bergendoff; architects Charles Moore and César Pelli; and landscape architect Angela Danadjieva.

When Woollen began working on the Children's Museum project in 1982, it must have felt like a particularly exciting commission. He had considerable experience in theater design, but museum projects – a plum commission for any architect – were far rarer in his portfolio. Years earlier, Woollen had been famously shut out of the running to design a new building for the Indianapolis Museum of Art, his public opposition to the museum's suburban relocation ruffling the feathers of the selection committee.[7] In the mid-1980s he would work on smaller renovation projects for regional museums like the Greater Lafayette Museum of Art and the Evansville Museum of Arts, History & Science. But the Children's Museum project was of a much larger scale and carried with it intriguing design opportunities.

Founded in 1925 by the civic reformer Mary Stewart Carey, the Children's Museum had grown over the decades to become a beloved city institution, the

Above:
Original museum entrance designed by Wright, Porteous and Lowe, 1976.

Below:
Children's Museum director Peter Sterling standing in the new museum lobby.

site of countless field trips and playdates for generations of Indianapolis youth. By the 1980s it was also the largest children's museum in the country, drawing more than a million visitors annually. Woollen's brief called for a multimillion-dollar addition to the museum's existing home, a dark-bricked behemoth designed only a decade prior by the local firm Wright, Porteous and Lowe. Its heavy, blocky architecture was not beloved; Philip Johnson had once allegedly dismissed it "a poor man's Pei" (a reference to the architect I. M. Pei).[8] Museum leaders needed more space and, with it, a personality shift – an architectural personality that might match the joyful exhibitions and educational activities for which the museum was best known.

Woollen's solution, which was primarily concentrated on the existing building's west end, was more than a Band-Aid. It transformed the museum's face into what the firm called a "gateway into the mind of a child. The child in all of us."[9] Working closely with Peter Sterling, the museum's director, Woollen zeroed in on the project's real client: young visitors themselves. The new museum needed to be "warm, inviting and friendly to a child," Woollen told the *Indianapolis News* in 1988 as construction was underway. "That's what we're trying to do, and that's what we'll be judged on."[10] At the same time, the design had to be more than just fun and games. The museum was a renowned educational institution, with a deep commitment to what Sterling called "minds on" learning. Play had to be balanced with purpose. "Children don't come here to feed on cream puffs. We are not a put-on. We offer real nutrition for the mind," Sterling said.[11]

To begin the project, the architects traded out their T squares for construction paper, crayons, and a blackboard. The team met with students and invited them to draw their ideal museum.[12] What did it look like? What types of activities could you do there? How did it make you feel? "The rule I make is that everyone is a collaborator," Woollen once said, and the Children's Museum project exemplified the architect's embrace of what's now known as participatory design.[13] As early as 1971 he had experimented with community charrettes (usually

Scott 8
Museum Store
Box Office

It's our 65th birthday —
celebrate with us all year long!
5
4

marathon sessions held over long weekends) as a means of public engagement, thereby letting some air into the normally hermetic design process.[14] Sometimes rowdy and unpredictable, they proved to be especially useful for the firm's many educational projects. During a planning workshop for a new library at St. Mary's College in northern Indiana, Woollen and the other adults in the room struggled to choose the building's location on campus. Then, a lone freshman offered an unlikely solution. "She finally picked up the symbol of the library and put it on a place and everybody drew in their breath because they knew it was the right one, and that's where it was built," remembered Woollen.[15]

In the Children's Museum workshop, some of the students drew conventional museum buildings, maybe like ones they had seen before. Others got more creative, imagining restaurants, slides, even helipads. Among other takeaways, these sessions convinced Woollen of the importance of a reimagined entry sequence – the architectural equivalent of a good first impression. This was no place for subtlety. "We were asked not to be contextual. We totally understood that our mission was to reverse feelings, to change the image and accommodate the users in a way never done before. I would be very hesitant about such a challenge if it had not been borne out by public reactions," he said about the project.[16] Back at the studio, the children's drawings inspired a series of whimsical design explorations for the building's reimagined facade. In one, an elephant's trunk doubled as a long hallway leading into the museum. In another, a boy's eyes were formed by two porthole windows.

While the final design was more conventional, a childlike irreverence toward scale, color, and

Study models for museum facade, ca. 1980s.

Water clock designed by Bernard Gitton installed in the new lobby, 1989.

proportion remained. Replacing the museum's previous entry sequence was now an almost comically monumental portico, gabled and held in place by four squat columns. Woollen had used front-facing gables extensively at Saint Meinrad, as well as in earlier projects like St. Luke's Episcopal Church and Indianapolis Public School no. 47 (now known as Edison School of the Arts), both in Indianapolis. An architectural historian would have recognized the museum's postmodern references and tasteful Palladian symmetry; to a younger eye, the museum was a colorful playhouse formed from the simple circles, squares, and triangles of a child's building blocks. Inside the arched facade Woollen placed a massive lunette window, its radial mullions extending up and out like a sun's rays. The window was trimmed in blue and green terra-cotta tile and stamped with the museum's name. Relief sculptures of carousel horses hinted at the fun waiting inside.

The new entrance introduced an entirely new architectural identity for the museum, but Woollen still remained sensitive to how this intervention knitted back into the original structure. "The hard problem was to do [the project] and not betray the old building. I firmly believe that the whole is more important than the parts."[17] In that spirit the portico was flanked on either side by wings built in the same brick palette as the Wright, Porteous & Lowe building. The left wing was rectangular and fronted by an exposed staircase. The right was serpentine, its wavy edifice softly mediating the transition between the original building's seriousness and the new entrance's pop exuberance. (A series of additions to the museum since have mostly obscured this aspect of Woollen's design.)

But perhaps the most significant change of all was what happened when one passed over the museum's new threshold. Where previously visitors had had trouble finding the building's front door, now they were welcomed into a cavernous four-story entry hall lit by skylights. "The effect is something like opening up a dungeon. It's recess. The prisoners dance in the sunlight," wrote Steve Mannheimer in his review of the building for the *Indianapolis Star*.[18] Banners emblazoned with children's drawings hung from exposed blue trusses. A towering water clock designed by the French artist Bernard Gitton transfixed young visitors with its Goldbergian intricacies. Finally, the shape of an elephant's trunk lived on in the form of a grand, curving staircase at the hall's far end. Lined with a yellow banister, it beckoned visitors in to the explore the building further like a friendly, outstretched hand. This is your museum, it seemed to say. Welcome.

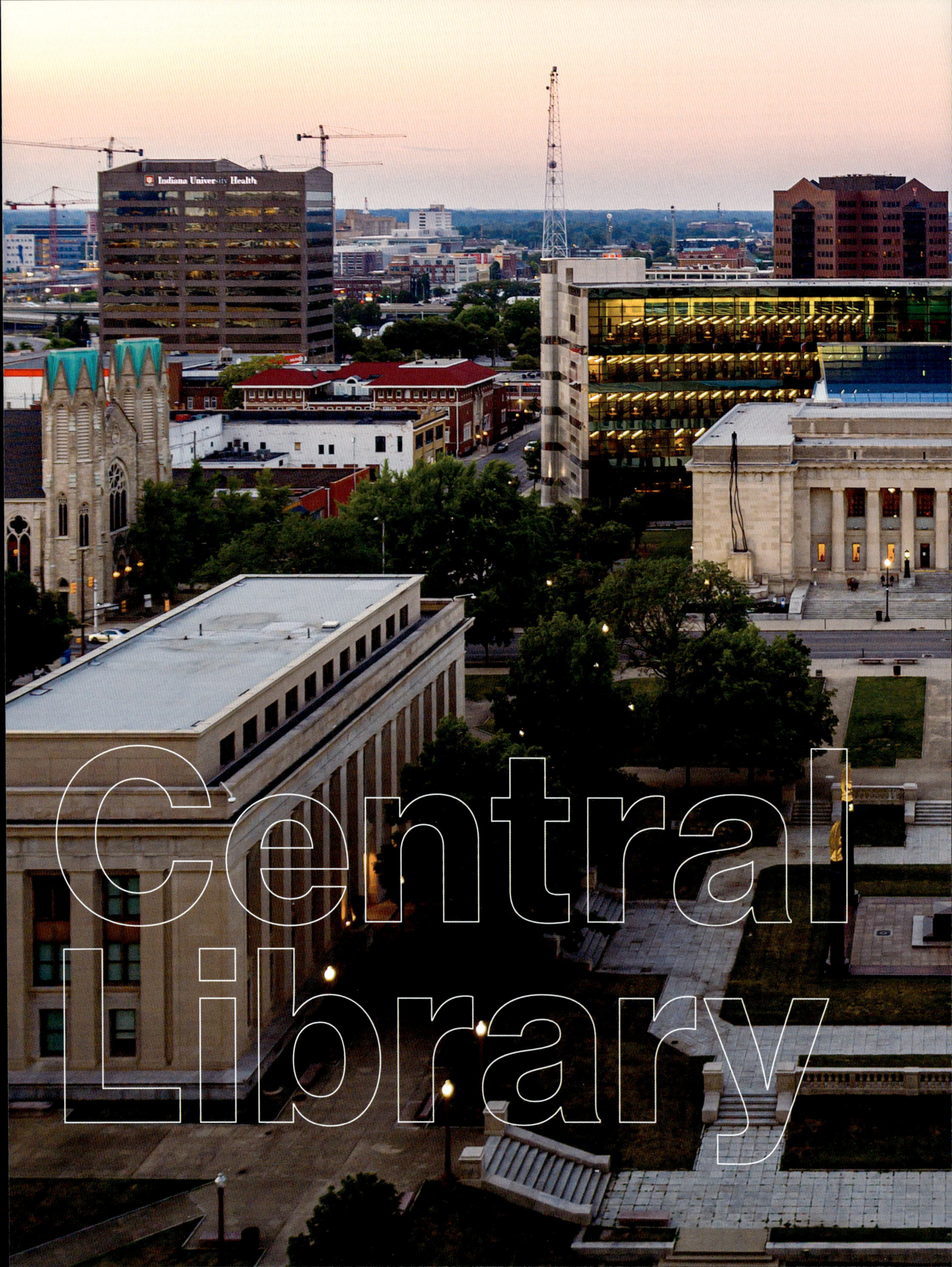

Central Library

Central Library addition, 2007.

Central Library

2007 | Indianapolis, IN

Woollen's career was dominated by two enduring interests: the creation of human-centered architecture and the elevation of Indianapolis's urban environment. The Central Library project brought those two interests together at spectacular scale. Consisting of a 237,000-square-foot addition to a ninety-year-old city landmark, Central Library was both the architect's last major work and one of the largest commissions of his entire career. "An enormous pleasure and at the same time a horrific responsibility," was how Woollen initially described the opportunity.[1] He would prove to be half-right.

In Indianapolis much has been written about the Central Library expansion and the maelstrom it inspired. Fifty million dollars over budget and two years behind schedule (the exact figures waffled depending on whom you asked), whatever Woollen achieved with the building architecturally was overshadowed by the many controversies left in its wake, a perfect storm of construction mismanagement, inept leadership, and financial blunder at taxpayers' expense. In 2004, with construction well underway, cracks the size of footballs were discovered in the building's concrete foundations. Work was suspended indefinitely while library leaders commissioned an independent investigation. A litany of additional problems soon surfaced, including the shocking revelation that the building's new underground parking garage was built six inches out of place.[2] Legal action – and a circular firing squad of blame – would follow, all breathlessly reported by the local press. "We're suing everybody," vowed one library official, and they did.[3] While the actual culpability of Woollen, Molzan and Partners for what appeared to be a construction failure remains a matter of debate, the firm was fired and sued for negligence. The parties settled out of court in 2006.

But even before the cracks were discovered, there had been turbulence. The Indianapolis-Marion County Public Library (now known as the Indianapolis Public Library) had long been a pillar of the city's civic life, and by 1995 nearly 70 percent of eligible residents were cardholders.[4] Many of them used Central Library, the system's largest, oldest, and most trafficked branch. But in the information era libraries were no longer just for books; as the organization's own mission statement put it, they were platforms for "community information services."[5] Reading and research coexisted with educational workshops, tutoring programs, self-help classes, and – above all – free internet access. In 1996 library leaders announced their intent to modernize Central Library to the tune of $23 million.

It was a hefty fee, and city politicians, fearing the partisan implications of a potential tax hike to pay for the project, balked. But the building sorely needed an update – and hadn't the government just helped the Indiana Pacers pay for a $183 million basketball stadium? "The mayor has obviously forgotten that a great city is measured not by its sporting events but by the level of services it provides its citizens," complained one of many letters published by the *Indianapolis Star*, referring to Mayor Stephen Goldsmith (the same mayor who had commanded the wrecking crew at Barton Tower a year before).[6] After much legal wrangling, library leaders finally got their way. On May 16, 1998, the *Indianapolis Star* announced Woollen as Central Library's new architect. The project was now described as a "significant addition" to the original building, and its budget doubled.[7] Its price tag would continue to climb over the next decade.

Woollen, now the *éminence grise* of Hoosier architecture, did not pitch for the project. In fact,

Indianapolis Central Library designed by Paul Philippe Cret, 1917, as seen from American Legion Mall.

he did not have to do much to win the project at all. The job was handed to him on a silver platter by Robert Kennedy, the library system's facilities manager. The former director of the city's planning department and an architect himself, Kennedy knew Woollen's work well, and the two had been friendly for decades. By Kennedy's logic, the rejuvenation of Central Library carried profound local significance. Who better than the "dean of Indiana architects" to take it on? "The board let me pick all the architects. As far I was concerned, he was the best architect in Indianapolis. He lived his entire life here. If you're working on an important building, you pick the best guy," remembered Kennedy.[8] The work was also a big deal for Woollen, Molzan and Partners' business, representing significant billings for a practice with a head count of less than twenty at the time. "It was a massive project, and it contained a lot of risk should something go wrong. And of course it did," remembered Kevin Huse, then serving as the firm's CEO.[9]

Woollen and his team got to work. They began by studying the existing structure, an extraordinary specimen of Beaux Arts architecture by the French American designer Paul Philippe Cret. Described as a "temple to a book" when it first opened in 1917 (on land donated, in part, by Hoosier poet James Whitcomb Riley), the neoclassical building stood at the northern terminus of the American Legion Mall, proudly announcing Indianapolis as a place of learning and knowledge for all.[10] Its plan was symmetrical in the Greek Revival style, distinguished by a central colonnaded facade and fine carvings inside and out. Woollen had long admired Cret as an architect, and Central Library was Cret "at his juiciest." He considered the building to be one of the last and finest remaining vestiges of the city's historic past. "I always take visiting architects to see it, and they gasp when they see the main reading rooms," he said.[11]

The commission also carried multiple layers of personal significance. Woollen's grandfather and namesake, Evans Woollen I, had helped to select the sixty-seven literary names carved into the original library building's exterior and interior walls.[12] In 1929

Evans I also helped commission the city's only other Cret-designed building, a school building for the John Herron Art Institute – to which Woollen also designed an addition, Fesler Hall, in 1962. Finally, Cret, a longtime faculty member of the University of Pennsylvania, had earlier been a mentor to Louis Kahn, Woollen's own teacher at Yale. All these factors likely weighed heavily on Woollen as the project unfolded.

As the needs for the new wing coalesced, it was clear that Woollen's addition would have to be highly considered. All agreed that the Cret building could not be materially changed. Any intervention would need to be additive in nature, respectful of its predecessor yet still fulfilling the library's needs for a modern facility with more space. The brief was like a tightwire on which Woollen was forced to balance: If the new wing was too loud or aggressive, it would suffocate Cret's design. Too modest, and the whole project risked collapsing under the good intentions of its own timidity. While some worried that the expansion's scope would strain what the city could financially accommodate, others – including Woollen – defended its ambition. "This is not a dream out of proportion to our city. We are just doing what would be expected of a city of our size," he said.[13]

From an architectural perspective, one of the most critical questions was scale. Although well proportioned for its function, Cret's library was not huge. In 1918 Ralph Adams Cram noted its somewhat diminutive size in a stirring review of the building for *Architectural Forum*. "To me the most notable qualities in the exterior are scale and surface. It is not a large building, yet the scale is so delicately preserved that one does not think of dimensions," he wrote.[14] Yet in the intervening years, the building's context had dramatically changed. Its surrounding neighborhood had matured, and the creation of the American Legion Mall in the 1920s meant that the library now commanded the head of one of the city's most dramatic open spaces – a situation Cret could not have predicted. "Dinky" was Woollen's own diagnosis of the building, and he sought to course correct.[15] He pursued a strategy that would significantly expand the library's spatial presence without overwhelming the original structure. It was the

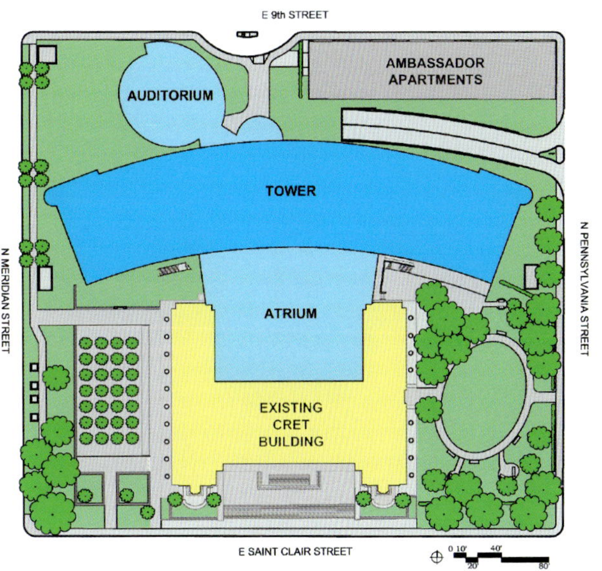

Library floor plan showing the addition.

same strategy he had followed decades earlier with Central Library's neighbor, the Minton-Capehart Federal Building: define the space, create containment, leave the city better than when you found it.

There was also the matter of style. Woollen's first library, the Marion College library completed in 1968, was a muscular work of brick and concrete Brutalism. But by the 1990s, he was designing almost exclusively in a postmodern vein, deeply inflected by classical precedent. As work began on Central Library, the firm was also finishing up another library, the Funk Agricultural, Consumer, and Environmental Sciences Library at the University of Illinois, which took its inspiration from the famous Radcliffe Camera of Oxford University built in 1749. A study model preserved in the firm's archives shows that Woollen explored a similarly historical design for Central Library. The model depicts a rectilinear addition of almost equal height as the Cret building, save for a glass-walled gable poking out like a cowlick on a bad haircut. The scheme was clearly not successful and likely confirmed for Woollen that a cleaner break with the past would be necessary. "To be a contextualist in this situation would mean you can't blow Cret up, literally, to this

BURNS
WORDSWORTH
SCOTT

LANIER
BIOGRAPHIES

indypl.org
The
INDIANAPOLIS PUBLIC
Library
Central Library

***Above*:**
Funk Agricultural, Consumer, and Environmental Sciences Library at the University of Illinois Urbana-Champaign, 2001.

***Below*:**
Model for early Central Library addition design, late 1990s.

type of scale. You have to stand back and be so respectful that you're not imitating Cret, we thought, after studying the whole thing," he said in 2002.[16]

The final design instead synthesized the full breadth of Woollen's architectural sensibilities – modernist and postmodernist, historic and futuristic, heroic and contextual, personal and public – in one harmonious scheme. This was Woollen at the height of his powers, deferential to the Cret building while still articulating an architectural statement befitting the project's iconic status. "A younger architect couldn't have done that building. They wouldn't have had that restraint," observed Huse.[17] For various reasons, the library's design is not widely known outside of Indianapolis. It was not covered in the national architectural press, and because of the legal fracas surrounding its completion, the firm did not submit it for architectural awards (which would have brought it more visibility). Compared to other large, urban public libraries such as Will Bruder Architects' Burton Barr Phoenix Central Library, Pei Cobb Freed's San Francisco Main Public Library, and OMA's Seattle Central Library, all completed in the late 1990s and early 2000s, Central Library is a design of noticeable simplicity, and by an architect with little to prove. For Woollen, it was a swan song to his city.

The addition's primary element was a minimalist glass-and-steel tower. Wide and gently parabolic, the tower cupped the old library from behind in an empathetic embrace. Its compressed profile allowed it to slip between the original Cret building and another existing structure on the site, an old apartment block called the Ambassador Building, which, after protests from neighborhood residents and preservationists, could not be moved.[18] Six stories tall, the new tower was much larger than either of these buildings, and filled with books, computer stations, and comfortable seating, it offered unparalleled views of downtown Indianapolis in every direction. Standing on the sixth floor, one could look south out onto American Legion Mall and into the heart of downtown Indianapolis, catching sight of both the Federal Building directly ahead as well as Barton Tower a few blocks east. Look north, and the density of the urban core disintegrated into more residential, near-downtown neighborhoods and commercial areas, with the Children's Museum of Indianapolis and Clowes Memorial Hall somewhere out in the distance.

Woollen often spoke about the tower in metaphors. It was "a foil" for the Cret building, "a kind of setting for the jewel" that maintained "the same sort of margins that you would find on the mat of a good picture."[19] Curiously, Woollen ignored the most obvious allusion: the tower looked like a giant open book, its glass-and-metal pages spread wide to envelop the Cret building in front of it. The allusion was obvious: this was a story about the past but written from the present. On the tower's east and west sides, stainless steel cladding provided an abrupt contrast to Cret's limestone facade. This reflective cladding was also used on a shorter, ovoid mass attached conspicuously (and unexpectedly) to the tower's northern face. The protrusion was something of a callback to the cylindrical prayer chapel of the New Harmony Inn, but here it housed a circular auditorium. The auditorium was underwritten by the Allen Whitehill Clowes Memorial Trust, a philanthropy funded by the estate of Woollen's old friend and patron who died in 2000.

Woollen was a passionate historic preservationist, but he was not opposed to tinkering with Cret's design when it suited him. The most obvious change was the removal of the rear chunk of Cret's building, a space that had formerly housed the library's stacks, to accommodate the tower's insertion. Its limestone façade, however, was saved, pushed inward to serve as an interior partition between the original building and the addition. On the building's opposite side, Woollen also made changes to the entrance design. Cret had designed a library with only one front door. Against the wishes of some historic preservationists, Woollen added a second and third door on either side of the original for additional points of egress. Woollen also demolished a more recent, 1976 addition on the library's west end. That addition, designed by Kennedy himself when he was in private practice, was known as the "silo" and was not loved by many. It broke the axial symmetry of Cret's original plan. Woollen restored it.

The tower connected to the original library via a seven-thousand-square-foot atrium. Primarily made of glass including its ceiling, this large and transparent space was something akin to an architectural bardo, mediating the transition between the neoclassical of Cret's library and the neocontemporary of Woollen's addition. Its spaciousness – ready-made for events, community gatherings, or simply meeting a friend for coffee – recalled similar grand foyers Woollen had created for Clowes Memorial Hall and the Children's Museum, but never had the architect achieved such weightlessness in so vast an area. In lieu of a bulky truss, slender steel columns arched majestically from floor to ceiling, casting languid shadows in their wake. The extensive use of glass was an obvious modernist gesture, a wink back to the glass box homes Woollen labored on a half century prior. Resplendent and infinitely programmable, this was the "big room concept" at a civic scale.

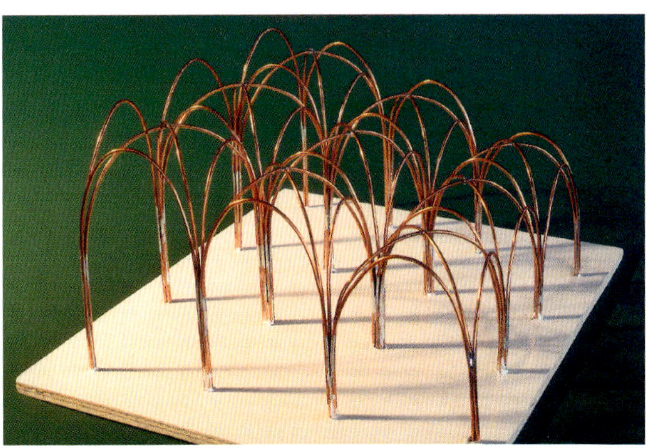

Study model showing atrium supports.

Central Library reopened on a snowy day in December 2007. Despite the near-freezing temperatures, it was a cause for celebration. Trumpeters led a procession of two thousand well-wishers into the new atrium. Mari Evans, the nationally known poet and longtime Indianapolis resident, recited "Paean for a New Library," written specifically for the occasion. "Welcome home," the library's board chair exclaimed to the assembled crowd. "This building is yours. Enjoy it in good health and go check out a book."[20] To provide an out-of-town imprimatur, the *Indianapolis Star* called in the critic Lawrence W. Cheek of the *Seattle Post-Intelligencer* to write an official review of the building. His evaluation was effusive and praised Woollen specifically: "Against all odds and logic, the new Central Library's appalling trail of botched construction, mind-boggling cost overruns, preposterous delays and volleying lawsuits has led to a stunningly good building."[21] It was likely the only time the newspaper ran an architectural review on its front page.

The building was a success. But for Woollen, the cost of that success was personal, a painful asterisk on what all believed would have been – should have been – a triumphant capstone to his entire career. "I really felt bad about what happened to him. He really put all he had into that building," remembered Kennedy later.[22] In the last years of his life, Woollen stayed mum about the project. The building went generally unmentioned in his 2010 lecture at the Indianapolis Museum of Art. In 2011 Woollen was the subject of a lengthy profile in *Indianapolis Monthly* magazine. Titled "The Pillar," the article was filled with the architect's usual pronouncements on all things architecture and Indianapolis. But when it came to discussing Central Library, Woollen turned taciturn. "It doesn't take much imagination to feel what it was like. But it's all part of life. And creation. It's never going to be easy," was all he said.[23]

Acknowledgments

This project was built on the generosity of many individuals over several years of work. First and foremost we thank Kevin Huse, former CEO of Woollen, Molzan and Partners, who embraced the idea from the start; Richard McCoy, executive director of Landmark Columbus Foundation, who gave us early encouragement and advice; and our editor at IU Press, Dan Crissman, who helped shape the project's final form. Thank you also to Steve Mannheimer who generously agreed to write the foreword for this book.

For sharing recollections of their time at Woollen Associates/Woollen, Molzan and Partners, thank you to Deborah A. Burkhart, Joe Burns, Dan Fogerty, Graham Greene, Ted Halsey, Mike Halstead, Kalevi Huotilainen, Louis Joyner, Peter Mayer, Jim McQuiston, Laurence O'Connor, Christopher Peragine, Erik Sueberkrop, Mark Van Allen, and Alan Weiskopf. We also thank Lee Alig, Bill Browne, Marsh Davis, Marc Dollase, Bob Kennedy, Steve Mannheimer, Jordan Ryan, and Ann Stack for their additional insight into Woollen's life and work.

For their knowledge of specific buildings (and in some cases answering a stranger's knock at the door), thank you to Denise Purdie Andrews; Bob Boeglin and Katherine Nagler; Jock Fortune; Fr. Harry Hagan, OSB; Krista Hall; Jeff Hindman; Elaine Howard; Meghan Hughes; Jerome Jacquard; G. B. Landrigan; Bob Lebow; Joan Leibman; Mary Ellen Meehan; Roger Naill; Kent Schuette; Greg and Flo Silver; Evan Solley; Adam Thies; Scott Tod; and Br. Stanley Rother Wagner, OSB.

In addition, thank you to Nick Alguire, Daniel Carlin, Aidan Cronin, Kevin Huse, Caroline Lee, Giorgia Lupi, Grant McCracken, Dana Newell, Sarah Pizer, and Becca Sanders for their comments on early versions of the manuscript.

This book is the first to comprehensively draw on the Woollen, Molzan and Partners corporate archive, a large collection of more than three thousand architectural drawings and ten thousand images now held by the Indiana Historical Society. Regan Steimel and her staff were essential to navigating this material, time and again accommodating our many requests. We are also indebted to Gayle O'Hara, formerly of the Special Collections, Rare Books, and University Archives at Butler University, for her help in locating records related to Clowes Memorial Hall and Irwin Library. For additional assistance, thank you to the staffs of the Avery Architectural & Fine Arts Library at Columbia University; Manuscripts and Archives at Yale University Library; Ruth Lilly Special Collections and Archives at Indiana University Indianapolis; University Archives at Indiana University Bloomington; Institute for Civic Leadership & Mayoral Archives at University of Indianapolis; Andrew Seager Archives of the Built Environment at Ball State University; Saint Meinrad Archabbey Archives; Indianapolis Public Library; Columbus Indiana Architectural Archives; US General Services Administration; and Prints and Photographs Division of the Library of Congress.

Finally, thank you to our families for their guidance and support along the way, and our parents for instilling curiosity and civic-mindedness as we grew up in Indianapolis.

List of Projects

Reconstructed from period photographs, press releases, award submissions, and newspaper announcements, this list begins to document the full output of Woollen's career. Dates generally correspond to building completion. Unbuilt projects are marked with an asterisk. We have intentionally omitted major projects attributed to Woollen, Molzan and Partners but completed without Woollen's involvement, such as White River Gardens (1999) and Indianapolis City Market (2010).

	Year	Name	Location
	1950	C. Beecher Hogan residence	St. Albans, VT
	1954	Paul Arlt residence	New Canaan, CT
	1954	Eugene J. Naill residence	New Canaan, CT
	1954?	Walker residence	Redding, CT
	1955	Thomas V. Parke residence	Indianapolis, IN
	1955	Lauriston C. Marshall residence	Indianapolis, IN
	1957	Frederick E. Meyer residence	Indianapolis, IN
	1957	AFNB Cumberland Branch	Cumberland, IN
(1)	1957	Hughes (James Thurston) residence	Indianapolis, IN
	1958	AFNB 42nd and College Branch renovation	Indianapolis, IN
	1958	Bertermann Floral Company interior design	Indianapolis, IN
	1958?	Calvin S. Hamilton residence	Indianapolis, IN
	1959	Louis Marks residence	Indianapolis, IN
	1959	Alexander Gerritsen residence	West Lafayette, IN
	1959	Abraham Lincoln Memorial*	IN
	1959	Fletcher Trust Building renovation	Indianapolis, IN
	1959	Merchants National Bank South 3rd Street Branch	Terre Haute, IN

(1)

(2)

(3)

	Year	Name	Location
	n.d.	Arnold Mason residence (*?)	Indianapolis, IN?
	1960	Delta Zeta sorority house	Greencastle, IN
(2)	1960	Sylvan Perlov residence	Indianapolis, IN
	1960	AFNB West Washington Branch	Indianapolis, IN
	1961	Frederick Hadley pool house	Indianapolis, IN
	1961	Phi Delta Theta fraternity house addition	Greencastle, IN
	1962	Fesler Hall, Herron School of Art	Indianapolis, IN
(3)	1962	AFNB Southport Branch	Southport, IN
	1963	Clowes Memorial Hall, Butler University	Indianapolis, IN
	1963	St. Thomas Lutheran Evangelical Church	Bloomington, IN
	1963	Warren Hills Christian Church	Indianapolis, IN
	1963	King of Glory Lutheran Church	Carmel, IN
	1964	Jordan and Joan Leibman residence	Indianapolis, IN
	1964	Donald M. Mattison residence	Indianapolis, IN
	1964	All Saints Episcopal Church addition	Indianapolis, IN
(4)	1964	Barron Mallory residence	Indianapolis, IN
	1964	American Institute of Architects Building (competition entry)*	Washington, DC
	1964	Indiana Credit Union League building	Indianapolis, IN
	1964	Asbury United Methodist Church	Indianapolis, IN
	1965	Lord of Life Lutheran Church	Indianapolis, IN?
	1966	Harry S. Wood High School Gymnasium	Indianapolis, IN
	1966?	Cummins Employee Recreation Association Building*	Columbus, IN
	1967	Ball State University Architecture Building (competition entry)*	Muncie, IN
	1967?	Benjamin Hitz Jr. residence	Indianapolis, IN
	1968	David Brower residence	Bloomington, IN
	1968	John J. Barton apartment building	Indianapolis, IN
(5)	1968	J. M. Rotz Engineering Co. building	Speedway, IN

(4)

(5)

(6)

	Year	Name	Location
	1969	St. Timothy's Episcopal Church	Indianapolis, IN
	1969	St. Thomas Aquinas Church	Indianapolis, IN
	1969	Downtown Churches Housing Corporation (apartment building)*	Bloomington, IN
(6)	1969	Red Geranium Refectory	New Harmony, IN
	1969	Michiana Place master plan*	South Bend, IN
(7)	1969	Yale University Mathematics Building (competition entry)*	New Haven, CT
	n.d.	Altoona Senior Citizens Housing*	Altoona, PA
	1970	Mother Theresa Hackelmeier Memorial Library, Marian University	Indianapolis, IN
	1970	Thomas T. Solley residence	Bloomington, IN
	1971	John J. Barton Annex	Indianapolis, IN
	1972	Musical Arts Center, Indiana University Bloomington	Bloomington, IN
	1972	Hoosier (Davlan) Apartments renovation	Indianapolis, IN
	1972	Indiana Credit Union League expansion*	Indianapolis, IN
	1972	Pruis (University) Hall, Ball State University	Muncie, IN
	1973	A. J. Thatcher Community Center	Indianapolis, IN
	1973?	Sprunica Elementary School addition	Nineveh, IN
	1973	Bissell Hall renovation, Hotchkiss School	Lakeville, CT
	1974	AFNB Franklin Road Branch	Lawrence, IN
	1974	Minton-Capehart Federal Building	Indianapolis, IN
	1975	Over-the-Rhine master plan and Pilot Center	Cincinnati, OH
	1975	Indiana University Purdue University Indianapolis (master plan)*	Indianapolis, IN
	1975	7-Up bottling factory	Indianapolis, IN
	1975	New Harmony Inn	New Harmony, IN
	1976	Strider Theater, Colby College	Waterville, ME
	1976	Tower Hill School master plan	Wilmington, DE
	1977	Banner-Graphic Building	Greencastle, IN
	1978	Solar Suites*	Indianapolis, IN

(7)

(8)

(9)

	Year	Name	Location
	1979	Westminster Village Retirement Center	Bloomington, IL
	1979	St. Andrew's School master plan	Middletown, DE
	1979	Watson Hall, Hotchkiss School	Lakeville, CT
	1980	White River Park Design Assistance Team (P/DAT) (master plan)*	Indianapolis, IN
	1980	Carol Woods Retirement Center	Chapel Hill, NC
(8)	1980	East Building, Indiana University Kokomo	Kokomo, IN
	1980	Indiana Repertory Theatre renovation	Indianapolis, IN
	1980	Majestic Building renovation	Indianapolis, IN
	1980	Union Station area master plan	Indianapolis, IN
	1981	Edsel Ford Memorial Library addition, Hotchkiss School	Lakeville, CT
	1982	Saint Meinrad Monastery and Library	Saint Meinrad, IN
	1982	Cushwa-Leighton Library, St. Mary's College	Notre Dame, IN
	1982	Indianapolis Public School no. 47	Indianapolis, IN
	1983	Main Building addition, Hotchkiss School	Lakeville, CT
	1983?	Atrium One elevated walkway	Cincinnati, OH
(9)	1984	Greater Lafayette Museum of Art addition*	Lafayette, IN
	1985	Evansville Museum of Arts, History & Science addition	Evansville, IN
	1985	Cultural center competition entry*	Muncie, IN
(10)	1986	St. Philip's Episcopal Church	Indianapolis, IN
	1986	Independence Square	Evansville, IN
	1986	Archibald residence	Isle au Haut, ME
	1986	Union Station renovation	Indianapolis, IN
	1986	St. Andrew Abbey Church	Cleveland, OH
(11)	1987	New Harmony Inn addition and conference center	New Harmony, IN
	1987	Judicial court building*	Indianapolis, IN
(12)	1988	Whitewater Valley Gorge master plan*	Richmond, IN
	1988	Moody Music Building, University of Alabama	Tuscaloosa, AL

(10)

(11)

(12)

	Year	Name	Location
	1989	Children's Museum of Indianapolis addition	Indianapolis, IN
	1989	Metairie Park Country Day School master plan and additions	Metairie, LA
	1989	Christ Church Cathedral addition and renovation	Indianapolis, IN
(13)	1989	St. Richard's School addition	Indianapolis, IN
	1992	St. Joseph County Public Library	South Bend, IN
	1994	Grainger Engineering Library, University of Illinois Urbana-Champaign	Urbana, IL
	1997	Saint Meinrad Archabbey Church renovation	Saint Meinrad, IN
	2001	Funk Agricultural, Consumer, and Environmental Sciences Library, University of Illinois Urbana-Champaign	Urbana, IL
	2002	Charles V. Park Library, Central Michigan University	Mount Pleasant, MI
	2003	Woollen residence	Lyons, CO
	2007	Central Library addition	Indianapolis, IN
	2008	Rosado Hill residence #1	Indianapolis, IN
(14)	2008	Rosado Hill residence #2	Indianapolis, IN
(15)	2008	Rosado Hill residence #3	Indianapolis, IN

(13)

(14)

(15)

Notes

Introduction

1. Will Higgins and Vic Ryckaert, "Architect Who Shaped City Dies," *Indianapolis Star*, May 19, 2016.
2. Evans Woollen, "Towards an Architecture of Process," *Arts & Architecture* 3, no. 4 (1985): 66.

How to Be a Good Architect

1. Evans Woollen, "To Build in Context," Indianapolis Museum of Art, June 3, 2010, YouTube, 42:04, https://www.youtube.com/watch?v=rIGc2SuwquU&t=2s.
2. Jim Morris, "Evans Woollen: The Man Behind the Landmarks," *Arts Indiana*, Summer 1994, 25.
3. Woollen, "To Build in Context."
4. Evans Woollen III Oral History Transcript, February 16, 2012, DVD 0573–0574, SC 3060, Indiana Historical Society, 8.
5. Harold Hartley, "Evans Woollen Jr. To Become Ranking U.S. Banker Tomorrow," *Indianapolis Times,* September 28, 1948.
6. Dan Wakefield, *New York in the 50s* (Orlando, FL: Houghton Mifflin Harcourt, 1992), 16. For more on Wakefield's relationship with Woollen, see Dan Wakefield, "All the Way Home: Author Dan Wakefield on Returning to Indianapolis," *Indianapolis Monthly,* October 2012, https://www.indianapolismonthly.com/arts-and-culture/dan-wakefield-all-the-way-home/. In *Going All the Way*, Wakefield also writes of a character named "Mrs. Hullen" who shares more than a passing resemblance to the Woollens. Dan Wakefield, *Going All The Way* (New York: Delacorte, 1970), 242.
7. Megan Fernandez, "The Pillar: Evans Woollen," *Indianapolis Monthly*, July 28, 2011, https://www.indianapolismonthly.com/arts-and-culture/circle-city/the-pillar-evans-woollen/.
8. Evans Woollen III Oral History Transcript, 8.
9. See Robert A. M. Stern and Jimmy Stamp, *Pedagogy and Place: 100 Years of Architecture Education at Yale* (New Haven: Yale University Press, 2016), 88–127.
10. Harriet G. Warkel, Martin F. Krause, and S. L. Berry, *The Herron Chronicle* (Indianapolis: Herron School of Art/Indiana University Purdue University Indianapolis, 2003), 22–23. Technically, Evans I was president of the Art Association of Indianapolis, which oversaw the Institute. He served for thirty-four years.
11. Robert Benson, "An Interview with Evans Woollen," *Inland Architect*, July/August 1987, 58.
12. Evans Woollen, interview by Esther McCoy, between 1964 and 1980, Esther McCoy papers, circa 1876–1990, Archives of American Art, Smithsonian Institution.
13. Evans Woollen, letter to Robert A. M. Stern, February 6, 1974, Reminiscences and Documentation of Architecture Students Collected by Robert A. M. Stern, RU 1001, Box: 4, Folder 96-97, Yale University Manuscripts and Archives. While Stern's original letter was not saved, he wrote to Woollen to request reminiscences about Yale in the 1950s for an article he was writing for the journal *Oppositions.* None of Woollen's insights made it into the final piece. Robert A. M. Stern, "Yale 1950–1960," *Oppositions* 4 (October 1974): 35–62.
14. Oral history interview with Yvonne Jacquette, October 19 and 21, 2010, Archives of American Art, Smithsonian Institution.
15. Stern and Stamp, *Pedagogy and Place*, 91; Roberto Gargiani, *Louis I. Kahn: Exposed Concrete and Hollow Stones: 1949–1959* (Lausanne: EPFL Press, 2014), 30.
16. "Student Architects, Painters, Sculptors Design Together," *Progressive Architecture,* April 1949, 18.
17. Esther McCoy, "Young Architects: The Small Office," *Arts & Architecture*, February/March 1966, 33.
18. Benson, "An Interview with Evans Woollen," 58.
19. In interviews Woollen most often cited his experience in Johnson's office. However, the résumé he submitted for the Clowes Memorial Hall commission also mentioned a previous "apprenticeship" with Johansen, his collaborator on the project. See letter and proposal from Johansen/Woollen Architectural Associates, 1959, Folder 3, Box 40, Clowes Family Collection, 1842–1998, Indiana Historical Society. Johansen is also mentioned in McCoy, "Young Architects," 33. However, another résumé from 1974 only mentions Gores alongside Johnson, omitting Johansen entirely. See Woollen, letter to Stern. Working in Gores's office is also discussed in "Clowes Conversations: The Architecture of Clowes Hall with Evans Woollen," January 30, 2014, YouTube, 55:53, https://www.youtube.com/watch?v=Aae6ED0eNMY&t=1142s.
20. Woollen, "To Build in Context."
21. "Woollen and Sewell Ceremony Is Today," *Indianapolis News,* July 16, 1955.
22. The address of the couple's first home was reported as 392 N. Delaware Street: "Woollen and Sewell Ceremony Is Today;" Connecticut Commission on Culture and Tourism, "Naill House," *New Canaan Mid-Century Modern Houses Appendices*, 2008, https://ncmodernist.org/2009.New.Canaan.Survey.Appendices.pdf, no page number.
23. Benson, "An Interview with Evans Woollen," 58. Woollen told Stern that the thesis was lost: Woollen, letter to Stern.
24. Charles Vaughan, "Architect Sees Duty to Help Home Town," *Indianapolis News,* November 19, 1962.

25. Philip J. Trounstine, "Evans Woollen: From Controversy, Effective Architecture," *Indianapolis Star Magazine,* May 8, 1976, 24. Trounstine references only four bank branches, however a review of archival material and newspaper announcements from the period suggests there may have been at least five: North College branch, West Washington branch, Southport branch, Cumberland branch, and Franklin Road branch.
26. Mike Brooks, "Woollen Favors a Multi-design City," *Indianapolis News*, September 25, 1967.
27. Projects featured in *Record*, *Forum*, or both are the Arlt house, Parke house, Delta Zeta sorority house, Merchants National Bank, Clowes Memorial Hall (cover story), Barton Tower, St. Thomas Aquinas Church, New Harmony Inn, Over-the-Rhine (cover story), Musical Arts Center, Watson Hall at the Hotchkiss School, St. Andrew Abbey, Saint Meinrad monastery, Indianapolis Public School no. 47, and the Children's Museum of Indianapolis.
28. Trounstine, "Evans Woollen: From Controversy, Effective Architecture," 18.
29. Trounstine, "Evans Woollen: From Controversy, Effective Architecture," 18.
30. "The Maestro: More Than An Architect–A Tribute to Lynn Molzan, FAIA," AIA Indianapolis, April 12, 2022, YouTube, 8:36, https://www.youtube.com/watch?v=PcG3th7JR-w.
31. Deborah A. Burkhart, interview with the authors, March 7, 2024.
32. Laurence O'Connor, interview with the authors, October 14, 2022.
33. James McQuiston, interview with the authors, November 26, 2023.
34. Steve Mannheimer, interview with the authors, April 12, 2023.
35. Peter Mayer, interview with the authors, June 30, 2023.
36. Graham Greene, interview with the authors, July 27, 2023.
37. Alan Weiskopf, interview with the authors, July 11, 2023.
38. "Is The City Doomed?" *Indianapolis Star Magazine,* March 29, 1953, 4.
39. Brooks, "Woollen Favors a Multi-Design City."
40. Trounstine, "Evans Woollen: From Controversy, Effective Architecture," 23.
41. Morris, "Evans Woollen: The Man Behind the Landmarks," 25.
42. Evie Birge, "Our City's Plus and Minus," *Indianapolis News,* August 20, 1963.
43. Trounstine, "Evans Woollen: From Controversy, Effective Architecture," 24.
44. Morris, "Evans Woollen: The Man Behind the Landmarks," 25.
45. White River Park Development Commission, "White River Park Master Plan," July 1, 1981, Folder 1, Box 2, OMB 160, Woollen, Molzan and Partners, Inc. Architectural Records, CA, 1912–2011, Indiana Historical Society. 22.
46. "Architecture: Showplace on the Prairie," *Time*, December 5, 1977, https://content.time.com/time/subscriber/article/0,33009,915780,00.html.
47. Nancy Kriplen, "Harry," *J. Irwin Miller: The Shaping of an American Town* (Bloomington: Indiana University Press, 2019), 79–89.
48. "The Cummins Foundation," Visit Columbus Indiana, https://columbus.in.us/wp-content/uploads/2016/07/Cummins-Foundation-Architecture-Program.pdf. In fact, the origins of the Cummins Foundation Architecture Program were rooted in a general dismissiveness towards Indianapolis's architectural talent. See Matt Shaw, *American Modern: Architecture, Identity, Columbus, Indiana* (New York: Monacelli, 2024), 90. In *Perspecta,* Will Miller, son of Irwin Miller, provides a thoughtful defense of the success of Columbus's "star system." "Will Miller," *Perspecta* 37 (2005): 138.
49. "Christian Theological Seminary, Board of Trustees and Advisory Council," Box 29, Richard G. Lugar Collection, Institute for Civic Leadership and Digital Mayoral Archives, University of Indianapolis.
50. The project is surprisingly absent from the Columbus Indiana Architectural Archives or the Cummins Foundation archives, two main repositories of Columbus-related architecture. The only apparent record is a few photographic slides saved in the Woollen, Molzan and Partners archive, now held by the Indiana Historical Society, and brief taped remarks Woollen made about the design to an audience of Ball State University architecture students in 1967. "Ceraland Park," Slide Box 10, Bins 15-16, Series 11, Woollen, Molzan and Partners, Inc. Architectural Records, CA. 1912–2011, Indiana Historical Society; Evans Woollen, "Architectural Design," Ball State University, May 15, 1967, YouTube, 1:04:20, https://www.youtube.com/watch?v=IgfCikwqOdo; O'Connor, interview with authors, 2022. It should be noted that in 1974 Woollen did appear on the foundation's shortlist of architects to design a new elementary school in the town of Taylorsville, north of Columbus, but his inclusion seems to have been a result of the community's request for more local architects rather than a sincere proposal by the foundation. In the end, the school board chose its own designer for the project, the first instance of a local entity rejecting the foundation's recommendation. See "Cummins Architect Rejected," *Republic,* February 5, 1975; Shaw, *American Modern,* 297–298. The authors thank Matt Shaw for his insight here.
51. Trounstine, "Evans Woollen: From Controversy, Effective Architecture," 24.
52. Steve Mannheimer, "Midwest Architects Prepare for Change," *Indianapolis Star,* December 5, 1982.
53. Benson, "An Interview with Evans Woollen," 61.
54. Kevin A. Drawbaugh, "Woollen Mark Seen on Major Indiana Buildings," *Indianapolis News*, February 16, 1988.
55. Robert Venturi, *Complexity and Contradiction in Architecture* (New York, Museum of Modern Art, 1966), 16.
56. There's some evidence that Woollen and Moore collaborated on early concepts for an ill-fated proposal for a new judicial building in downtown Indianapolis, but the exact extent of that partnership is unclear. Kevin Callahan, "Design Justice, Hoosier Style," *Inland Architect,* July/August 1987, 32.
57. Benson, "An Interview with Evans Woollen," 59.
58. Kalevi Huotilainen, interview with the authors, March 20, 2024.
59. "Pilot Center–Filling in Over-the-Rhine," *Architectural Record,* October 1975, 81–86.
60. Evans Woollen, "Towards an Architecture of Process," *Arts & Architecture* 3, no. 4, 66.
61. Whitehead's "process philosophy" was influential to many architects, including Mies and Johnson. It's not clear when Woollen first discovered Whitehead, but it may have been as early as the 1950s during his time at Yale. In 1951, George Howe, chairman of the Yale Department of Architecture, gave a lecture to the school community in which he quoted Whitehead liberally. His remarks were subsequently published in *Perspecta*, giving them further currency. George Howe, "Training for the Practice of Architecture," *Perspecta* 1 (Summer 1952): 2–7.

62. Morris, "Evans Woollen: The Man Behind the Landmarks," 25.
63. Ted Halsey, interview with the authors, March 28, 2023.
64. Woollen, "To Build in Context."

Parke House

1. "The Big Room Concept," *Architectural Record*, May 1957, 117.
2. Glenn Fowler, "Space at a Given Cost – Four Architects Offer Their Solutions," *New York Times*, October 27, 1957.
3. James A. Jacobs, *Detached America: Building Houses in Postwar Suburbia* (Charlottesville: University of Virginia Press, 2015), 133–168.
4. Evans Woollen, "To Build in Context," Indianapolis Museum of Art, June 3, 2010, YouTube, 42:04, https://www.youtube.com/watch?v=rIGc2SuwquU&t=2s.
5. Lesley Jackson, *Contemporary: Architecture and Interiors of the 1950s* (New York: Phaidon, 1994), 87–88.
6. Russell Lynes, "The American at Home – 1957," *Architectural Record*, May 1957, 100.
7. Robert Benson, "An Interview with Evans Woollen," *Inland Architect,* July/August 1987, 58. While Woollen does not refer to the residence by name, he mentions it was published by *Architectural Record* in 1955, indirectly identifying it as the Arlt house: "Five Approaches to the Sloping Site," *Architectural Record*, February 1955, 171. See also Connecticut Commission on Culture and Tourism, "Evans Woollen III," *New Canaan Mid-Century Modern Houses Appendices*, 2008, G40. https://ncmodernist.org/2009.New.Canaan.Survey.Appendices.pdf.
8. Evans Woollen, interview with Esther McCoy, between 1964 and 1980. Esther McCoy papers, circa 1876–1990. Archives of American Art, Smithsonian Institution.
9. "Evans Woollen III," *New Canaan Mid-Century Modern Houses Appendices*, 2008, G40.
10. Woollen, interview with McCoy.
11. Paul C. Diebold, "Single-Family Residential Architecture," *Encyclopedia of Indianapolis,* 1994, https://indyencyclopedia.org/single-family-residential-architecture/.
12. See Connie Zeigler, "'Living Furiously': The Design Life of Avriel Shull," *Traces of Indiana and Midwestern History* 24, no. 4 (Fall 2012): 17–27.
13. The Herron exhibition was evidently influential for one visitor, the local businessman Harry E. Berke. Berke would remember Mies's work from the show and commission him to design two office buildings in Indianapolis, neither of which were built: Dietrich Neumann, *Mies van der Rohe: An Architect in His Time* (New Haven: Yale University Press, 2024), 317.
14. "Landscaped Wooded Lot Setting For Concrete Home Constructed By H. L. Horton Co. in North Indianapolis," *Indianapolis Star,* June 27, 1937.
15. "$5,500," *Indianapolis Star,* September 19, 1937.
16. "House in North Kessler Manor, Indianapolis, IN," *Architectural Forum*, June 1938, 510.
17. Shannon L. Hill, "The Indianapolis Home Show: Its History, Evolution, and Centerpiece Homes" (master's thesis, Ball State University, May 2002), 35–36. As Hill documents, some of these model homes (including the modern ones) were eventually erected in Indianapolis neighborhoods.
18. "Indianapolis Architects Play Key Role at 1958 Home Show," *Indiana Architect*, April 1958.
19. "Fine Formality under $20,000," *House & Garden's Book of Buildings*, Fall–Winter 1958–1959, 58. The home is also known as the Thurston house after its original owner, James S. Thurston.
20. Meghan Hughes, interview with the authors, June 7, 2023.
21. "Delta Zeta Sorority House," *Indiana Architect*, October 1960, 11–12. The project was also featured in *Architectural Forum*, erroneously attributed to "Evans Woolen." "Sorority House, De Pauw [*sic*] University," *Architectural Forum*, November 1960, 148–149.
22. Corbin Patrick, "Future Is for People Who Live in Glass Houses," *Indianapolis Star*, July 21, 1960.
23. Ann Rein, "Architect Points Out Necessity of 'Heart' in Home," *Indianapolis News*, March 17, 1960.
24. "Japanese Influence Is Designed into Contemporary Home," *Indianapolis Star*, March 5, 1961.
25. "Wrapped Up in Itself," *House & Garden Magazine*, May 1963, 156.
26. *Building for Meaning: The Architecture of Evans Woollen* (documentary) (Indianapolis: Spellbound Productions, 1994). Plans for the Lucas house were published in Philip Johnson, "Whence & Whither: The Processional Element in Architecture," *Prospecta* 9/10 (1965): 175.
27. Esther McCoy, "Young Architects: The Small Office," *Arts & Architecture*, February/March 1966, 28.
28. *Building for Meaning*, 1994.
29. Joan Leibman, interview with the authors, October 29, 2023.
30. Anne P. Robinson and S. L. Berry, *Every Way Possible: 125 Years of the Indianapolis Museum of Art* (Indianapolis: Indianapolis Museum of Art, 2008), 146–149.
31. "Donald M. Mattison House," National Register of Historic Places Registration Form, US Department of the Interior, May 20, 2020.
32. Kevin A. Drawbaugh, "Woollen Mark Seen on Major Indiana Buildings," *Indianapolis News*, February 16, 1988.

Clowes Memorial Hall

1. Robert Gover, "'Culture' Comes to Indianapolis," *New York Times Magazine*, December 24, 1967, 6.
2. "Series Internationale," *Indianapolis Star*, August 25, 1963.
3. Edna Folz, "Clowes Hall Expected to Serve 'Any Need,'" *Evansville Press*, August 17, 1963.
4. Gover, "'Culture,'" 12.
5. Program, procedural notes laying of cornerstone Clowes Hall, November 24, 1961, Folder 6, Box 40, Clowes Family Collection, 1842–1998, Indiana Historical Society.
6. See "Why Not a Civic Auditorium?," *Indianapolis Star*, June 17, 1947; Corbin Patrick, "Our Old Theater Gone but Is Not Forgotten," *Indianapolis Star*, June 12, 1955; Marshall Lincoln, "Clowes Hall Urged as Cultural Agency Link," *Indianapolis News*, November 21, 1961. The idea of a new auditorium was also present in "Central Business District Report," Metropolitan Planning Department, 1958, https://citybase-cms-prod.s3.amazonaws.com/67edcb3392fe4d8382c3d52f5f9e43bd.pdf.
7. Alexander W. Clowes, *The Doc and the Duchess: The Life and Legacy of George H. A. Clowes* (Bloomington: Indiana University Press, 2016), 148.
8. Angelo Angelopolous, "Clowes Hall Stone Laying Called Milestone for the Arts," *Indianapolis News,* November 25, 1961. This was likely a reference to the "Acropolitan Area"

promoted by Kurt Panzer: Anne P. Robinson and S. L. Berry, *Every Way Possible: 125 Years of the Indianapolis Museum of Art* (Indianapolis: Indianapolis Museum of Art, 2008), 144.

9. “Clowes Family Gives Butler Auditorium,” *Indianapolis News*, May 29, 1959.
10. Evans Woollen, “To Build in Context,” Indianapolis Museum of Art, June 3, 2010, YouTube, 42:04, https://www.youtube.com/watch?v=rIGc2SuwquU&t=2s.
11. “Clowes Conversations: The Architecture of Clowes Hall with Evans Woollen,” January 30, 2014, YouTube, 55:53, https://www.youtube.com/watch?v=Aae6ED0eNMY&t=1142s.
12. Evans Woollen, interview by Esther McCoy, between 1964 and 1980, Esther McCoy papers, circa 1876–1990, Archives of American Art, Smithsonian Institution.
13. Gover, “‘Culture,’” 11.
14. Letter and proposal from Johansen/Woollen Architectural Associates, 1959, Folder 3, Box 40, Clowes Family Collection, 1842–1998, Indiana Historical Society.
15. “Clowes Conversations.” According to Woollen, local firm McGuire & Shook was also interviewed: Woollen, interview by Esther McCoy, between 1964 and 1980.
16. “Enabling Resolution Adopted by the Executive Committee of Butler University on June 30, 1959, and Approved by the Board of Directors on November 4, 1959,” Folder 18, Box 10, Buildings and Grounds Collection, Special Collections, Rare Books, and University Archives, Irwin Library, Butler University.
17. This description comes from an early draft of the article Woollen would write for *Arts & Architecture,* which was edited by McCoy. The Clowes passage was ultimately edited out of the final text. Evans Woollen, “Towards an Architecture of Process,” 1984, Box 14, Folder 25, Esther McCoy papers, circa 1876–1990, Archives of American Art, 4–5.
18. Indeed, this slab is labeled as “marquee” on the building’s blueprints. “Clowes Memorial Hall Blueprints,” 1960, FF21-D, Clowes Family Collection, 1842–1998, Indiana Historical Society.
19. See Joan Ockman, “The School of Brutalism: From Great Britain to Boston (and Beyond),” in *Heroic: Concrete Architecture and the New Boston*, ed. Mark Pasnik, Michael Kubo, and Chris Grimley (New York: Monacelli, 2015), 30–47.
20. John Johansen, “Act and Behavior in Architecture,” *Perspecta* 7 (1961): 49. Renderings of the Clowes project (misspelled as “Cowles”) were included in the *Perspecta* article, but Woollen was not cited as coarchitect.
21. Thelma Machael, “Clowes Hall Blends Past and Present,” *Indianapolis News*, October 10, 1963.
22. Rosanna Hall, “Clowes Hall Concrete Shocks and Fascinates,” *Indianapolis News,* September 7, 1963.
23. “Clowes Conversations,” 2014.
24. Woollen, interview by Esther McCoy, between 1964 and 1980.
25. “Enabling Resolution.”
26. “Executive Committee Meeting,” October 29, 1959, Folder 12, Box 6, Board of Trustees Papers, 1850–2012, Special Collections, Rare Books, and University Archives, Irwin Library, Butler University.
27. Board documentation shows that the trustees considered a short list of architects – Edward Larrabee Barnes; Philip Johnson; Skidmore, Owings & Merrill; and Yamasaki – who were recommended to them by Saarinen and Pietro Belluschi, then dean of MIT’s architecture school. Miller had previously turned to Saarinen and Belluschi for advice on selecting architects for projects in Columbus, suggesting it was he who also organized this process for the Butler trustees. “Meeting of Board of Directors,” April 15, 1959, Folder 11, Box 6, Board of Trustees Papers, 1850–2012, Special Collections, Rare Books, and University Archives, Irwin Library, Butler University.
28. “Special Meeting of Board of Directors,” August 10, 1960, Folder 18, Box 10, Buildings and Grounds Collection, Special Collections, Rare Books, and University Archives, Irwin Library, Butler University.
29. Megan Fernandez, “The Pillar: Evans Woollen,” *Indianapolis Monthly*, July 28, 2011, https://www.indianapolismonthly.com/arts-and-culture/circle-city/the-pillar-evans-woollen/.
30. “Clowes Conversations.”
31. “Memorandum Regarding the Very Preliminary Study for a Lincoln Memorial in Indiana,” July 22, 1959, Folder OBC030, Rare Books and Manuscripts, Indiana State Library.
32. It may have been an early proposal for a project that was ultimately given to the Indianapolis architect Edward D. Pierre, but Pierre’s design also went unbuilt. See Jill York O’Bright, “There I Grew Up . . .”: A History of the Administration of Abraham Lincoln’s Boyhood Home,” *National Park Service*, 1987, https://www.nps.gov/parkhistory/online_books/libo/adhi/adhi4.htm. Various sketches in the Pierre archive at Ball State University seem to confirm this: “Sketch for Monument with Covered Wagon,” Pierre & Wright Architectural Records Collection, 3-176.4A, Andrew Seager Archives of the Built Environment, Ball State University. See also Michael A. Capps, “Interpreting Lincoln – A Work in Progress: Lincoln Boyhood National Memorial as a Case Study,” *Indiana Magazine of History* 105, no. 4 (2008): 336.
33. Marc D. Allan, “In His Own Words: Architect Evans Woollen,” *Butler Magazine*, Summer 2013.
34. Betsy Brockway, “Styles Splendid, Stately,” *Indianapolis Star*, October 19, 1963.
35. Gover, “‘Culture,’” 11.
36. “Many-Faceted Stage for the Performing Arts,” *Architectural Forum*, December 1963, cover; “Ten Buildings That Point the Future,” *Fortune*, October 1964, 137.
37. “Brightness in the Air,” *Time*, December 18, 1964, 56.
38. Evans Woollen, “Letters,” *Time,* January 1, 1965, 8.

Barton Tower

1. Kevin O’Neal, “City Wants Barton Annex to Be Housing of Choice, Not Chance,” *Indianapolis News*, February 28, 1994.
2. Michele McNeil, “Pacer-Painted Wrecking Ball Doesn’t Bounce the City’s Way,” *Indianapolis News*, June 1, 1995.
3. Steve Mannheimer, “Barton Apartments Renovators Might Trip over Curb Appeal,” *Indianapolis Star*, March 20, 1994.
4. Mike Brooks, “Woollen Favors a Multi-design City,” *Indianapolis News*, September 25, 1967.
5. “The Elderly of Massachusetts Avenue,” Box 056, The Richard G. Lugar Collection, Institute for Civic Leadership and Digital Mayoral Archives, University of Indianapolis, 3; Joan Hostetler, “Then & Now: Millikan Flats / Barton Tower / Millikan on Mass, 500 Block of Massachusetts Avenue,” *Historicindianapolis.com,* December 6, 2012, https://historicindianapolis.com/indianapolis-then-and-now-millikan-flats-barton-tower-millikan-on-mass-500-block-of-massachusetts-avenue/.

6. "Descriptive Data, AIA Honor Awards Program 1969," Box 2, Folder 17, Woollen, Molzan and Partners, Inc. Architectural Records, CA. 1912–2011, Indiana Historical Society.
7. "High-Rise Home for Oldsters Will Be Ready by Next Spring," *Indianapolis Star*, August 20, 1967; David Mannweiler, "10 Buildings Will Add 112 Stories," *Indianapolis News*, January 5, 1968.
8. Evans Woollen, "Architectural Design," Ball State University, May 15, 1967, YouTube, 1:04:20, https://www.youtube.com/watch?v=IgfCikwqOdo. The title of this talk is listed elsewhere as "Radiant City Revisited."
9. William A. Browne Jr., "The Ralston Plan: Naming the Streets of Indianapolis," *Traces of Indiana and Midwestern History* 25, no. 3 (Summer 2013): 8–9.
10. "A Brief History of Indianapolis," Box 14, Richard G. Lugar Collection, Institute of Civic Leadership and Digital Mayoral Archives, University of Indianapolis.
11. "Our City and How It Proposes to Pay for Its Seven Year Plan of Improvements," ISLO 336, no. 47, Pamphlet Collection, Indiana Division, Indiana State Library. See also Jon C. Teaford, *Indianapolis: A Concise History* (Bloomington: Indiana University Press, 2024), 125–127.
12. "Our City and How It Proposes to Pay for Its Seven Year Plan of Improvements." Woollen's father's name is listed on page 42.
13. Mary Ellen and Mark Murphy, "The Cities of America: Indianapolis," *Saturday Evening Post*, August 7, 1948, 114.
14. US Census data as cited in "Suburbanization," *Encyclopedia of Indianapolis*, https://indyencyclopedia.org/atlas/pop/.
15. *Indianapolis Centrum: Design Potential Study*, March 1968, 12/2/815, Student Studies, 1965–, University Archives, University of Illinois at Urbana-Champaign; Michael J. Quinn, "White River 'Dream Town' Recommended," *Indianapolis Star*, March 24, 1968. The plan also received attention from the Chicago magazine *Inland Architect* in A. Richard Williams's "Cities of the Future," April 1967, 14. Woollen is listed as a "visiting critic" for the project, which was perhaps how he became aware of it. Later, the *Star*'s editorial page urged Mayor Richard Lugar to take the proposal seriously: "Challenge by the Riverside," *Indianapolis Star*, March 31, 1968.
16. Woollen, "Architectural Design."
17. See Teaford, *Indianapolis*, 128; "Indianapolis Goes It Alone," *Architectural Forum*, September 1960, 130–133. Unfortunately a full history of Indianapolis's postwar development has yet to be written.
18. Mannweiler, "10 Buildings Will Add 112 Stories."
19. Thomas A. Keating, "Zebrowski Destroys – But with Flair," *Indianapolis Star*, June 1, 1969.
20. "A New Horizon for Indianapolis . . . Riley Center Apartments," *Indianapolis Star Magazine*, May 19, 1963. See also Libby Cierzniak, "The Day the H-Bomb Hit Downtown Indy," Indypolitan.com, October 28, 2020, www.indypolitan.com/post/the-day-the-h-bomb-hit-downtown-indy. Part of Riley Center's appeal was its intentional recreation of suburban life: "Today's New Cities within Cities," *House & Home*, April 1962, 143–157.
21. Charles Vaughan, "Architect Sees Duty to Help Home Town," *Indianapolis News,* November 19, 1962.
22. *Indiana Architect*, May 1963, cover. For a report on protests against the project see Charles S. Preston, "No Jimcrow in Swank Project, NAACP Warns," *Indianapolis Recorder*, October 28, 1961.
23. Harrison J. Ullman, "Is High-Rise Housing the Answer?," *Indianapolis Star*, October 29, 1967.
24. Evans Woollen, "If Cities Prevail," *Indiana Architect*, November 1966, 16; Louis I. Kahn, "The Room, the Street, and Human Agreement," *AIA Journal* 56, no. 3 (September 1971): 33. Woollen also quoted a similar statement by Kahn in documentation for his work on the Union Station master plan: "Urban Design Concept," Union Station Master Plan/Indianapolis, 1980, Folder 1, Box 15, Woollen, Molzan and Partners, Inc. Architectural Records, CA, 1912–2011, Indiana Historical Society.
25. "Barton Tower Addition Set," *Indianapolis News*, February 19, 1969.
26. "The Elderly of Massachusetts Avenue," 10, 23.
27. "Happiness for Oldsters Is Living in New High-Rise Apartments," *Indianapolis Star*, May 26, 1968.
28. John Dixon, "Palazzo Vecchio, Indiana Style," *Architectural Forum*, November 1968, 71.
29. Richard Lugar to Evans Woollen, December 6, 1969, Task Force on Housing Correspondence 1968, Box 075, Richard G. Lugar Collection, Institute for Civic Leadership and Digital Mayoral Archives, University of Indianapolis.
30. "Architecture," *United States Pavilion Japan World Exposition 1970*, United States Information Agency, https://www.state.gov/wp-content/uploads/2019/04/Osaka-Expo-1970-Guidebook.pdf. The photograph of Barton can be seen in situ on page 22. The exhibition was curated by Ivan Chermayeff with the input of Peter Blake, editor-in-chief of *Architectural Forum.*
31. G. E. Kidder Smith, *The Architecture of the United States: An Illustrated Guide to Notable Buildings*, vol. 2 (Garden City: Anchor/Doubleday, 1981), 250.
32. Ullman, "Is High-Rise Housing the Answer?"
33. Ullman, "Is High-Rise Housing the Answer?"
34. Woollen, "Architectural Design."
35. Nonetheless, "The Barton Towers are a bright spot and serve a crying need. Success should receive HUD funding priority." Quoted in "The Elderly of Massachusetts Avenue," Box 056, The Richard G. Lugar Collection, Institute for Civic Leadership and Digital Mayoral Archives, University of Indianapolis.
36. Curt Ailes, "Barton Tower Expansion: Socially Just?," *UrbanIndy.com*, December 5, 2012, https://urbanindy.com/2012/12/05/barton-tower-expansion-socially-just/.

St. Thomas Aquinas Church

1. Evans Woollen, interview with Esther McCoy, between 1964 and 1980, Esther McCoy papers, circa 1876–1990. Archives of American Art, Smithsonian Institution.
2. Dan Carpenter, "St. Thomas Aquinas Catholic Church – Celebrating 75 Years," *St. Thomas Aquinas Church and School*, May 18, 2014. https://www.staindy.org/church/history/.
3. Philip Allen, "St. Thomas Church Design Primitive," *Indianapolis News*, March 7, 1970.
4. "A Church for the Revised Catholic Liturgy," *Architectural Record*, February 1970, 120.
5. "St. Thomas Aquinas Church Project Description," Box 2, Folder 9, Woollen, Molzan and Partners, Inc. Architectural Records, CA, 1912–2011, Indiana Historical Society.
6. Peter Mayer, interview with the authors, June 30, 2023.
7. Robert Benson, "An Architecture of Engagement: The Work of Evans Woollen," *Inland Architect*, July/August 1987, 58.

8. For an excellent study of this topic, see Gretchen Buggeln, *The Suburban Church: Modernism and Community in Postwar America* (Minneapolis: University of Minnesota Press, 2015). For a history of Indianapolis religious architecture, see Joseph M. White, "Religious Architecture," *Encyclopedia of Indianapolis*, January 1994. https://indyencyclopedia.org/religious-architecture/.
9. "Piety in Brick," *Time*, January 27, 1941. https://time.com/archive/6603584/religion-piety-in-brick/.
10. Fremont Power, "Seminary Is Severe, But Warm," *Indianapolis News*, April 4, 1966.
11. Woollen, interview with McCoy, between 1964 and 1980.
12. Buggeln, *Suburban Church*, 130–131.
13. For Kahn's use of hexagons, particularly in religious projects, see Sarah Williams Goldhagen, *Louis Kahn's Situated Modernism* (New Haven, CT: Yale University Press, 2001), 64–101.
14. "Unto You Is Born . . . a Savior," *Indianapolis News*, December 16, 1961; "Lutheran Church," *Arts & Architecture,* April 1962, 27.
15. Woollen, interview with McCoy, between 1964 and 1980.
16. Mayer, interview with authors.
17. Philip J. Tounstine, "Evans Woollen: From Controversy, Effective Architecture," *Indianapolis Star Magazine,* May 8, 1976, 20.

Musical Arts Center

1. Nancy Kriplen, "The Opera Factory," *Opera News*, November 1984, 16.
2. "Indiana's Elegant New 'Opera Factory,'" *Architectural Record*, February 1973, 120.
3. "Indiana's Elegant New 'Opera Factory,'" 119.
4. "Proposal for a Musical Arts Center," December 1965, C145.22, University Chancellor Herman B Wells Administrative Records, Indiana University Archives, Bloomington.
5. See George M. Logan, *The Indiana University School of Music: A History* (Bloomington: Indiana University Press, 2000), 177–228.
6. "An Ode to Airplane Hangar," *Terre Haute Tribune*, February 11, 1968.
7. "Proposal for a Musical Arts Center."
8. Elvis J. Stahr and Herman B Wells, letter to Dr. and Mrs. Herman C. Krannert, August 25, 1966, C145.22, University Chancellor Herman B Wells Administrative Records, Indiana University Archives, Bloomington.
9. Elvis J. Stahr and Herman B Wells, letter to Mr. Randall Tucker, July 12, 1965, C145.22, University Chancellor Herman B Wells Administrative Records, Indiana University Archives, Bloomington.
10. See Jacob Hardesty, "Building the 'Opera Factory': Elsie Irwin Sweeney's Philanthropic Leadership in Funding the Indiana University Music Arts Center," in *Women at Indiana University: 150 Years of Experiences and Contributions*, ed. Andrea Walton (Bloomington: Indiana University Press, 2022), 362–383.
11. J. Terry Clapacs with Susan Moke, Dina Kellams, and Carrie Schwier, "Musical Arts Center: Grand Performance Venue," *Indiana University Bloomington: America's Legacy Campus* (Bloomington: Indiana University Press, 2021), 80–83.
12. "Appointment of Architects; Change in Eggers and Higgins Contract," Indiana University Board of Trustees minutes, January 14–15, 1965, https://webapp1.dlib.indiana.edu/iubot/view?docId=1965-01-14.xml&chunk.id=d1e119&toc.depth=1&toc.id=d1e119&brand=iubot&text1=woollen&op1=and&op2=and&field1=text&field2=text&field3=text&fromYear=1965&startDoc=1#.
13. Herman Wells, letter to Evans Woollen, March 16, 1965, C145.22, University Chancellor Herman B Wells Administrative Records, Indiana University Archives, Bloomington.
14. Bill Pittman, "Musical Arts Center '1st' 'Spots' Architect," *Indianapolis News*, January 28, 1972.
15. Evans Woollen, "Architectural Design," Ball State University, May 15, 1967, YouTube, 1:04:20, https://www.youtube.com/watch?v=IgfCikwqOdo.
16. Charles Staff, "All's on Grand Scale at Musical Arts Center," *Indianapolis News*, September 16, 1971.
17. Ruth Mullen, "Warm and Welcoming," *Indianapolis Star*, February 3, 2001.
18. Pittman, "Musical Arts Center."
19. Kriplen, "Opera Factory," 116.
20. Al Ensen and Evans Woollen, "A Sculpture by Henry Moore for the New Opera House at IU," letter to Herman B Wells, May 28, 1968, C145.22, University Chancellor Herman B Wells Administrative Records, Indiana University Archives, Bloomington.
21. The $180,000 quote appears to have corresponded to the larger of two models Moore proposed for the MAC commission, which Woollen preferred. Evans Woollen to Herman B Wells, "Re: Indiana University Musical Arts Center," August 2, 1968. Pushback to the commission came from administrator Paul Klinge, who told Wells he had discussed the matter with Bain at length. Paul Klinge to Herman B Wells, "Moore sculpture," September 30, 1968, C145.22, University Chancellor Herman B Wells Administrative Records, Indiana University Archives, Bloomington.
22. John Fancher, "Arts Center a Dream Come True for Dr. Bain," *Herald-Times*, January 16, 1972.
23. Evans Woollen and Herman B Wells, transcript, October 1, 1970, C145.22, University Chancellor Herman B Wells Administrative Records, Indiana University Archives, Bloomington.
24. Staff, "All's on Grand Scale."
25. Suzanne Seed, "Bloomington's Astonishing Music School," *Chicago Tribune Magazine*, July 9, 1972, 28; Michael Steinberg, "Heracles: An Opera Premier," *Boston Globe*, July 18, 1972.

Federal Building

1. Philip J. Trounstine, "Evans Woollen: From Controversy, Effective Architecture," *Indianapolis Star Magazine,* May 8, 1976, 20.
2. Merle Edington, "Psychedelic Monstrosity," *Indianapolis Star*, October 6, 1975.
3. E. L. M., "Federal Building Has Right Design," *Indianapolis News*, December 11, 1973.
4. Megan Fernandez, "The Pillar: Evans Woollen," *Indianapolis Monthly*, July 28, 2011, https://www.indianapolismonthly.com/arts-and-culture/circle-city/the-pillar-evans-woollen/.
5. "1978 ISA Biennial Awards Program Descriptive Data," Box 2, Folder 21, Woollen, Molzan and Partners, Inc. Architectural Records, CA, 1912–2011, Indiana Historical Society.
6. Evans Woollen, "To Build in Context," Indianapolis Museum of Art, June 3, 2010, YouTube, 42:04, https://www.youtube.com/watch?v=rIGc2SuwquU&t=2s.
7. Christopher Peragine, interview with the authors, August 11, 2023.

8. Jon C. Teaford, *Indianapolis: A Concise History* (Bloomington: Indiana University Press, 2024), 133–150; Nicole Poletika, "The Undemocratic Making of Indianapolis," *Belt Magazine*, March 29, 2019, https://beltmag.com/undemocratic-indianapolis-unigov-poletika/.
9. Terry Curry, "Federal Building Dedicated," *Indianapolis News,* October 24, 1974.
10. See Nathan Glazer, "Daniel P. Moynihan and Federal Architecture," in *From a Cause to a Style: Modernist Architecture's Encounter with the American City* (Princeton, NJ: Princeton University Press, 2007), 146–162.
11. Connie Zeigler, "Minton-Capehart Federal Building," *Society of Architectural Historians*, https://sah-archipedia.org/buildings/01-097-0094.
12. "Federal Building to Stand Atop Arcade," *Indianapolis Star,* February 2, 1967; "Federal Building On 'Stilts,'" *Indianapolis News,* February 2, 1967.
13. Erik Sueberkrop, interview with the authors, May 19, 2023.
14. Likely inspired by a similar program in Cincinnati, Urban Walls only produced two murals, the second of which was coincidentally designed by James McQuiston. In an awards submission statement for the Federal Building, Woollen referred to the Federal Building's mural as an "Urban Wall," perhaps suggesting he considered Glaser's work part of this larger effort. "1978 ISA Biennial Awards Program Descriptive Data," Box 2, Folder 21, Woollen, Molzan and Partners, Inc. Architectural Records, CA, 1912–2011, Indiana Historical Society.
15. Donald W. Thalacker, *The Place of Art in the World of Architecture* (New York: Chelsea House, 1980), 69; Fred D. Cavinder, "The Colors and the Controversy," *Indianapolis Star*, June 23, 1983.
16. Janet Schneider, "A Revolutionary Artist's Rainbow," *Indianapolis Star*, December 15, 2011.
17. A little-known poster Glaser designed for the Shadowlight Theatre a few years prior did employ a similar gradient technique, but *Color Fuses* represented an entirely different scale. Beth Kleber, "The Glaser Nobody Knows: 2 Milton Posters for Kappo Phelan's Shadowlight Theatre," *Print*, https://www.printmag.com/graphic-design/the-glaser-nobody-knows-2-milton-posters-for-kappo-phelan-s-shadowlight-theatre/.
18. Thalacker, *Place of Art,* 69.
19. John H. Lyst, "Federal Building Displays Happy Face to Visitors," *Indianapolis Star*, December 3, 1974.
20. Cavinder, "The Colors and the Controversy."
21. Schneider, "Revolutionary Artist's Window."
22. Trounstine, "Evans Woollen: From Controversy, Effective Architecture," 23.
23. Trounstine, "Evans Woollen: From Controversy, Effective Architecture," 24.

New Harmony Inn

1. Donald E. Pitzer and Josephine M. Elliott, "New Harmony's First Utopians, 1814–1824," *Indiana Magazine of History* 75, no. 3 (September 1979): 227; Michael J. Lewis, "Harmony," in *City of Refuge: Separatists and Utopian Town Planning* (Princeton, NJ: Princeton University Press, 2016), 131–168.
2. Herb Marynell, "New Harmony Inn Reflects History," *Evansville Press*, May 1, 1974.
3. Gerald M. Allen, "New Harmony Inn: A Triumph of Modesty," *Architectural Record*, April 1976, 102. Portions of Allen's review were subsequently reprinted in Charles Moore and Gerald Allen, "Modesty: If It's Not the End, It's Certainly the Beginning," in *Dimensions: Space, Shape & Scale in Architecture* (New York: Architectural Record, 1976), 157–166.
4. Larry Pond, "New Harmony to Get New 35-Unit Motel," *Evansville Press*, May 15, 1969.
5. Stephen Fox, "Patronage and Modernism," in *Avant-Garde in the Cornfields: Architecture, Landscape, and Preservation in New Harmony*, ed. Ben Nicholson and Michelangelo Sabatino (Minneapolis: University of Minnesota Press, 2019), 139–163.
6. Jane Blaffer Owen, *New Harmony, Indiana: Like a River, Not a Lake: A Memoir* (Bloomington: Indiana University Press, 2015), 150.
7. Christine Gorby, "The New Harmony Gardens of Jane Blaffer Owen," in *Avant-Garde in the Cornfields: Architecture, Landscape, and Preservation in New Harmony*, ed. Ben Nicholson and Sabatino Michelangelo (Minneapolis: University of Minnesota Press, 2019), 238.
8. See Cammie McAtee, "'The Ribcage of the Human Heart,'" in *Avant-Garde in the Cornfields*, 105–169; Bob Hauton, "'So the Spirit May Prevail,'" *Evansville Press*, February 14, 1960. Owen and Johnson's relationship was tumultuous; see Barbara Grizzuti Harrison, "Life's Simple Treasures: Jane Blaffer Owen Seeks and Funds Paradise on Earth," *Vanity Fair*, August 1983, https://archive.vanityfair.com/article/1983/8/lifes-simple-treasures. Harrison quotes Owen as saying the church's design process was a battle of wills: "'If you want to build like that, dear Philip, then you must take your Bauhaus school design to Is-ra-el and build a nuclear reactor. It is against nature not to have curves.' So I took Philip Johnson over the hills and dales for which he was grateful." For Johnson's (very different) side of the story, see Mark Lamster, *The Man in the Glass House: Philip Johnson, Architect of the Modern Century* (New York: Little, Brown, 2018), 272–275.
9. Robert Benson, "An Interview with Evans Woollen," *Indiana Architect*, July/August 1987, 58.
10. "Recent Work of Evans Woollen," *Architectural Record*, May 1967, 139.
11. Marynell, "New Harmony Inn Reflects History."
12. *Building for Meaning: The Architecture of Evans Woollen* (documentary) (Indianapolis: Spellbound Productions, 1994).
13. The spiral staircase recalls those used in the Parke and Leibman homes, as well as an interior renovation job for a store in Indianapolis. Filomena Gould, "Staircase Focal Point in New Bertermann's," *Indianapolis News*, November 18, 1958. Gould wrote that "the architect tells me that he could be called an addict where these staircases are concerned."
14. The chapel is mentioned as an element of the inn's first design in Pond, "35-Unit Motel."
15. See Reyner Banham, *A Concrete Atlantis: U.S. Industrial Building and European Modern Architecture* (Cambridge, MA: MIT Press, 1986), 11–15.
16. Allen, "New Harmony Inn," 105.
17. Ben Nicholson, "The New Harmony Atheneum: White Collage," in *Avant-Garde in the Cornfields*, 264–266.
18. Harrison, "Life's Simple Treasures."
19. Christine Gorby, "An Evolving Commemorative Environment," in *Avant-Garde in the Cornfields*, 93.
20. "The New Harmony Athenaeum: Richard Meier Interviewed by Ben Nicholson. March 25th, 2010, New York," *Archinect*,

January 2, 2011, https://archinect.com/features/article/102847/the-new-harmony-athenaeum-richard-meier-interviewed-by-ben-nicholson-march-25th-2010-new-york.
21. *Building for Meaning*, 1994.

Saint Meinrad Monastery

1. Responses to "General Program Document Questionnaire," Building Committee: Questionnaire Volumes 1–3, 1982 Monastery/Library Construction, Saint Meinrad Archabbey Archives.
2. "Steering Committee for New/Renovated Monastery, Meeting of June 1, 1977, Guest Speaker: The Rev. Michael Komechak, OSB, Consultant from St. Procopius Abbey," 1982 Monastery/Library Construction, Saint Meinrad Archabbey Archives.
3. "Statement of Monastic Life," August 24, 1977, 1982 Monastery/Library Construction, Saint Meinrad Archabbey Archives.
4. *Building for Meaning*, 1994.
5. Margaret Gaskie, "Continuity Amid Change," *Architectural Record*, April 1985, 131.
6. Evans Woollen, "Towards an Architecture of Process," *Arts & Architecture*, 1985, 67.
7. Fr. Killian, Responses to "General Program Document Questionnaire," Building Committee: Questionnaire Volumes 1–3, 1982 Monastery/Library Construction, Saint Meinrad Archabbey Archives.
8. Christopher Peragine, interview with the authors, August 11, 2023.
9. Fr. Harry Hagan, OSB, interview with authors, August 13, 2023.
10. Fr. Harry Hagan, OSB, interview with authors, August 13, 2023.

Children's Museum of Indianapolis

1. The Fantus Co., Inc., "An Investor's Profile of Indianapolis," January 31, 1972, Box 57, Richard G. Lugar Collection, Institute of Civic Leadership and Digital Mayoral Archives, University of Indianapolis, 65.
2. David Mannweiler, "Apple Just for Opener," *Indianapolis News*, January 22, 1982; James Sholly, "Move Over New York – Apple Is Our Middle Name: A Case for the Independent Exploration of Regional Design Histories," in *After the Bauhaus, Before the Internet: A History of Graphic Design Pedagogy*, ed. Geoff Kaplan (Cambridge, MA: No Place Press, 2022), 340.
3. Ralph D. Gray, *IUPUI—The Making of an Urban University* (Bloomington: Indiana University Press, 2003), 44.
4. IUPUI Master Plan, Folder 2, Box 2, OMB 160, Woollen, Molzan and Partners, Inc. Architectural Records, CA, 1912–2011, Indiana Historical Society, 27.
5. Gray, *IUPUI*, 252.
6. "P/DAT Report," February 15–18, 1980, Folder 7, Box 14, Woollen, Molzan and Partners Architectural Collection, Indiana Historical Society, 28.
7. Philip J. Trounstine, "Evans Woollen: From Controversy, Effective Architecture," *Indianapolis Star Magazine,* May 8, 1976, 23; Anne P. Robinson and S. L. Berry, *Every Way Possible: 125 Years of the Indianapolis Museum of Art* (Indianapolis: Indianapolis Museum of Art, 2008), 146–149. Although no documentation of it exists, Woollen briefly describes his counterproposal for the art museum in unpublished remarks made to Esther McCoy: Evans Woollen, interview with Esther McCoy, between 1964 and 1980. Esther McCoy papers, circa 1876–1990. Archives of American Art, Smithsonian Institution.
8. Steve Mannheimer, "Children's Museum Grows Up Handsomely," *Indianapolis Star*, October 2, 1988.
9. "1990 AIA Honor Awards Program Descriptive Data," Folder 19, Box 5, Woollen, Molzan and Partners, Inc. Architectural Records, CA, 1912–2011, Indiana Historical Society.
10. Kevin A. Drawbaugh, "Woollen Mark Seen On Major Indiana Buildings," *Indianapolis News,* February 16, 1988.
11. Rex Redifer, "This House Serves Up 'Nutrition for the Mind,'" *Indianapolis Star*, October 2, 1988.
12. A recording of one session exists in the firm's archive. Videotape Storage, Box 1, Woollen, Molzan and Partners, Inc. Architectural Records, CA, 1912–2011, Indiana Historical Society.
13. Evans Woollen, "Learning from the Practice," May 8, 2002, Ball State University, YouTube, 1:13:37, https://www.youtube.com/watch?v=LhylMobAJn0.
14. Marvin E. Rosenman, "Charrette: A Real Way to Learn," *AIA Journal*, July 1971, 48.
15. Evans Woollen, "To Build in Context," Indianapolis Museum of Art, June 3, 2010, YouTube, 42:04, https://www.youtube.com/watch?v=rIGc2SuwquU&t=2s.
16. Robert Benson, "An Architecture of Engagement: The Work of Evans Woollen," *Inland Architect*, July/August 1987, 56–57.
17. Mannheimer, "Children's Museum Grows Up Handsomely."
18. Mannheimer, "Children's Museum Grows Up Handsomely."

Central Library

1. Evans Woollen, "Learning from the Practice," Ball State University, April 8, 2002, YouTube, https://www.youtube.com/watch?v=LhylMobAJn0.
2. Kevin Corcoran, "A $153M Mess," *Indianapolis Star*, July 23, 2006.
3. Lori Lovely, "Indianapolis Central Library Project Plagued by Calamities," *Construction Equipment Guide*, January 17, 2006, https://www.constructionequipmentguide.com/indianapolis-central-library-project-plagued-by-calamities/6546.
4. "Expanding Our Horizons: Indianapolis-Marion County Public Library Annual Report–1995," as cited in S. L. Berry with Mary Ellen Gadski, *Stacks: A History of the Indianapolis-Marion County Public Library* (Indianapolis: Indianapolis-Marion County Public Library Foundation, 2011), 198.
5. "Into the 21st Century: Indianapolis-Marion County Public Library 1996 Annual Report," as cited in Berry, *Stacks*, 199.
6. Kenneth J. Falk, "Library Project," *Indianapolis Star*, June 8, 1997.
7. Steve Mannheimer, "Architect Opens Chapter on Library," *Indianapolis Star*, May 16, 1998.
8. Robert Kennedy, interview with the authors, March 31, 2023.
9. Kevin Huse, interview with the authors, October 28, 2022.
10. "Riley Spirit Marks Library Dedication," *Indianapolis News*, October 8, 1917.
11. Woollen, "Learning from the Practice."
12. Lawrence J. Downey, *A Live Thing in the Whole Town: The History of the Indianapolis-Marion County Public Library, 1873–1990* (Indianapolis: Indianapolis-Marion County Public Library Foundation, 1991), 37.
13. Sally Falk Nancrede, "Huge Library Addition Goes on Display," *Indianapolis Star*, June 14, 2000.
14. Ralph Adams Cram, "The Indianapolis Public Library," *Architectural Forum*, September 1918, 67.

15. "Evans Woolen [*sic*], Architect of Transformed Central Library in Indianapolis," Indianapolis Public Library, December 12, 2012, YouTube, 8:18.
16. Woollen, "Learning from the Practice."
17. Huse, 2022.
18. So contentious was the preservation of the Ambassador Building that Kennedy, a proponent of the building's relocation, resigned in protest. Berry, *Stacks*, 208.
19. Woollen, "Learning from the Practice."
20. Berry, *Stacks*, 221.
21. Lawrence W. Cheek, "Architecture Critic Says New Library Deserves 'a Whoop of Joy,'" *Indianapolis Star*, December 9, 2007.
22. Kennedy, interview with the authors, March 31, 2023.
23. Megan Fernandez, "The Pillar: Evans Woollen," *Indianapolis Monthly*, July 28, 2011, https://www.indianapolismonthly.com/arts-and-culture/circle-city/the-pillar-evans-woollen/.

Photo Credits

Page	Credit
iv	© The Indianapolis Star – USA Today Network.
vi	Woollen, Molzan and Partners Architectural Collection, Indiana Historical Society.
viii–ix	Woollen, Molzan and Partners Architectural Collection, Indiana Historical Society.
2	Peter Mayer.
6	Woollen, Molzan and Partners Architectural Collection, Indiana Historical Society.
8	Woollen, Molzan and Partners Architectural Collection, Indiana Historical Society.
10	Roger Naill.
12	Woollen, Molzan and Partners Architectural Collection, Indiana Historical Society.
13	© The Indianapolis Star – USA Today Network.
14	Woollen, Molzan and Partners Architectural Collection, Indiana Historical Society.
15	Woollen, Molzan and Partners Architectural Collection, Indiana Historical Society.
15	Andrew Seager Archives of the Built Environment, Ball State University, Muncie, IN.
16	Indiana Convention and Visitors Association, Indiana Historical Society.
16	Indiana Convention and Visitors Association, Indiana Historical Society.
17	Woollen, Molzan and Partners Architectural Collection, Indiana Historical Society.
18	Woollen, Molzan and Partners Architectural Collection, Indiana Historical Society.
18	Woollen, Molzan and Partners Architectural Collection, Indiana Historical Society.
19	Library of Congress, Prints and Photographs Division, Balthazar Korab Collection, Korab F4408, item number 36.
19	Woollen, Molzan and Partners Architectural Collection, Indiana Historical Society.
20	Woollen, Molzan and Partners Architectural Collection, Indiana Historical Society.
20	*Inland Architect.*
20	Woollen, Molzan and Partners Architectural Collection, Indiana Historical Society. Photograph by Balthazar Korab.
22	© Robert Kittila.

Page	Credit
28	Woollen, Molzan and Partners Architectural Collection, Indiana Historical Society.
30	© The estate of Pedro E. Guerrero. Woollen, Molzan and Partners Architectural Collection, Indiana Historical Society.
32	Woollen, Molzan and Partners Architectural Collection, Indiana Historical Society.
38	Hedrich-Blessing Collection, Chicago History Museum. Photograph by Bill Engdahl. HB-23347-B. Woollen, Molzan and Partners Architectural Collection, Indiana Historical Society.
40	Getty Research Library, Los Angeles (980060). © J. Paul Getty Trust.
44	Photograph by Art Shay. © Richard Shay.
46	Buildings and Grounds Collections, Special Collections, Rare Books, and University Archives, Irwin Library, Butler University Libraries.
46	Clowes Family Collection, 1842–1998, Indiana Historical Society. Illustration by Jock Bevan.
47	Woollen, Molzan and Partners Architectural Collection, Indiana Historical Society.
49	Woollen, Molzan and Partners Architectural Collection, Indiana Historical Society.
49	Woollen, Molzan and Partners Architectural Collection, Indiana Historical Society.
60	Buildings and Grounds Collections, Special Collections, Rare Books, and University Archives, Irwin Library, Butler University Libraries.
60	W. H. Bass Photo Company Collection, Indiana Historical Society.
61	Indiana State Library.
62	Annette Brattinga.
66	City of Indianapolis, Department of Metropolitan Development, Indiana Historical Society.
66	City of Indianapolis, Department of Metropolitan Development Indiana Historical Society.
68	George Cserna photographs and papers, 1937–1978, Drawings and Archives Dept., Avery Architectural and Fine Arts Library © Columbia University in the City of New York. Woollen, Molzan and Partners Architectural Collection, Indiana Historical Society.
69	Woollen, Molzan and Partners Architectural Collection, Indiana Historical Society.
69	Woollen, Molzan and Partners Architectural Collection, Indiana Historical Society.
76	W. H. Bass Photo Company Collection, Indiana Historical Society.
78–79	Andrew Seager Archives of the Built Environment, Ball State University, Muncie, IN.
82–83	Images of the University of Illinois Archives, RS 12/2/815, Box 1, Item "Indianapolis Centrum Design Potential Study."
84	Woollen, Molzan and Partners Architectural Collection, Indiana Historical Society.
85	George Cserna photographs and papers, 1937–1978, Drawings and Archives Dept., Avery Architectural and Fine Arts Library © Columbia University in the City of New York. Woollen, Molzan and Partners Architectural Collection, Indiana Historical Society.
85	Woollen, Molzan and Partners Architectural Collection, Indiana Historical Society.
90	Woollen, Molzan and Partners Architectural Collection, Indiana Historical Society. Photograph by Balthazar Korab.

Page	Credit
92	Woollen, Molzan and Partners Architectural Collection, Indiana Historical Society.
93	Woollen, Molzan and Partners Architectural Collection, Indiana Historical Society. Photograph by Balthazar Korab.
93	Woollen, Molzan and Partners Architectural Collection, Indiana Historical Society.
100	Peter Mayer.
100	Woollen, Molzan and Partners Architectural Collection, Indiana Historical Society.
101	Woollen, Molzan and Partners Architectural Collection, Indiana Historical Society.
104	Woollen, Molzan and Partners Architectural Collection, Indiana Historical Society. Photograph by Balthazar Korab.
106	Courtesy of Indiana University Archives. Rendering by Helmut Jacoby.
106	Courtesy of Indiana University Archives. Illustration by Eggers and Higgins.
107	Courtesy of Indiana University Archives.
122	Woollen, Molzan and Partners Architectural Collection, Indiana Historical Society.
128	Woollen, Molzan and Partners Architectural Collection, Indiana Historical Society.
130	Woollen, Molzan and Partners Architectural Collection, Indiana Historical Society.
130	Indiana State Archives, Walker and Weeks Collection, Accession #1999482, Box 128.
131	Institute for Civic Leadership and Mayoral Archives University of Indianapolis.
140	Woollen, Molzan and Partners Architectural Collection, Indiana Historical Society. James McQuiston.
141	Milton Glaser estate
144	Woollen, Molzan and Partners Architectural Collection, Indiana Historical Society. Photograph by Balthazar Korab.
146	Woollen, Molzan and Partners Architectural Collection, Indiana Historical Society.
147	Woollen, Molzan and Partners Architectural Collection, Indiana Historical Society.
158	Meier Partners.
163	Woollen, Molzan and Partners Architectural Collection, Indiana Historical Society.
165	Woollen, Molzan and Partners Architectural Collection, Indiana Historical Society. Photograph by Balthazar Korab.
165	Woollen, Molzan and Partners Architectural Collection, Indiana Historical Society.
174	Woollen, Molzan and Partners Architectural Collection, Indiana Historical Society. Photograph by Balthazar Korab.
176–177	© Tim Hursley.
178	© Tim Hursley.
180	Woollen, Molzan and Partners Architectural Collection, Indiana Historical Society.
181	Woollen, Molzan and Partners Architectural Collection, Indiana Historical Society.

Page	Credit
181	The Children's Museum of Indianapolis and the IU Indianapolis University Library Digital Collections.
182	© Tim Hursley.
183	The Children's Museum of Indianapolis and the IU Indianapolis University Library Digital Collections.
184	Woollen, Molzan and Partners Architectural Collection, Indiana Historical Society.
184	Woollen, Molzan and Partners Architectural Collection, Indiana Historical Society.
184	Woollen, Molzan and Partners Architectural Collection, Indiana Historical Society.
184	Woollen, Molzan and Partners Architectural Collection, Indiana Historical Society.
185	The Children's Museum of Indianapolis and the IU Indianapolis University Library Digital Collections.
190	W. H. Bass Photo Company Collection, Indiana Historical Society.
191	Woollen, Molzan and Partners Architectural Collection, Indiana Historical Society.
204	University of Illinois at Urbana-Champaign Archives, image acecitcs-03067cbr.tif, Record Series 8/1/57.
204	Woollen, Molzan and Partners Architectural Collection, Indiana Historical Society.
205	Woollen, Molzan and Partners Architectural Collection, Indiana Historical Society.
212	Woollen, Molzan and Partners Architectural Collection, Indiana Historical Society.
213	Woollen, Molzan and Partners Architectural Collection, Indiana Historical Society.
214	Woollen, Molzan and Partners Architectural Collection, Indiana Historical Society.
215	Woollen, Molzan and Partners Architectural Collection, Indiana Historical Society.

Phillip Cox is a writer and native Hoosier. He lives in New York City, where he worked for the design firm Pentagram.

Niall Cronin is a photographer in New York City. Born in Indianapolis, his work has been shown at the Indianapolis Museum of Contemporary Art (iMOCA) and Edington Gallery. He's been published in the *Financial Times*, *Fast Company*, and *Time Out*.

For Indiana University Press

Sabrina Black *Editorial Assistant*
Tony Brewer *Artist and Book Designer*
Gary Dunham *Acquisitions Editor and Director*
Anna Francis *Assistant Acquisitions Editor*
Anna Garnai *Production Coordinator*
Samantha Heffner *Marketing and Publicity Manager*
Katie Huggins *Production Manager*
David Miller *Lead Project Manager/Editor*
Dan Pyle *Online Publishing Manager*
Pamela Rude *Senior Artist and Book Designer*